Heart OF Stone

JOURNEY TO THE HEART OF THE HOLY SPIRIT

RACHEL GODFREY

ENDORSED BY J OAN HUNTER

T.N.T. Publishing
Oakdale, Louisiana

Endorsements

"From A Heart of Stone" is the personal testimony of a beautiful soul. In a very real sense, her journey is everyone's journey. Rachel Godfrey chronicles her personal discoveries of life in the spirit, healing, ministering deliverance from evil spirits, visions of Jesus, intimate worship, giving and receiving prophetic words and words of knowledge, and the impartation of spiritual gifts down generational lines. Her experiences can be a doorway for you to enter into the supernatural life God always meant you to possess. Read, enjoy, and expect God to act in your life also.

-Joan Hunter
Author/Evangelist, Joan Hunter Ministries
www.joanhunter.org

Rachel Godfrey's passion is birthed from her understanding of religion vs relationship. She has a personal perspective of religious life without the Holy Spirit compared to life and relationship with the Holy Spirit. In this book, she takes you through her beginning journey of discoveries and adventures with her best friend.

If you are hungry for more and desperate to have a relationship with God, then this book is an honest and vulnerable account of getting to know and trust God through a relationship with the Holy Spirit. The book will challenge you, inspire you, and encourage you to connect with God in ways you may have never thought.

-Phillip Hand
Founder, Vision House Ministries, England
www.vhm.org.uk

Rachel is a prime example of how when we live in the spirit and release control of man, miracles really do happen. She demonstrates the willingness to live her life guided by the Holy Spirit - A faith filled life. It is my prayer that as you read her book, these words will lead you to God's word and that you will also find your righteous path.

-Barbara Rucci
Co-Founder/Vice President, Double Portions Ministries.
www.dpministries.net

This manuscript is inspiring. God's stamp of approval is on this book.

-Alfred Hernandez, M.A.Ed.
Professor/Editor

"From A Heart of Stone" is a remarkable compilation of Rachel's amazing encounters with Holy Spirit. Her candid and engaging writing style will grip the heart of readers to pursue their own personal, unique relationship with The Godhead. As Rachel did, allow Holy Spirit to overshadow your analytical thinking and reasoning as He takes you on a journey into His heart. Your life will forever be changed.

-Courtney Bowers-Artiste
Author/Publisher/Founder, Fully Persuaded Ministries
www.pastorcourtney.net

A book destined to change lives. Rachel's unique and rich blend of medical expertise, scriptural/Biblical knowledge, and real-life testimonies dare the reader to internalize the message of healing. *From a Heart of Stone* reveals the sheer joy and depth of the heart that wrote it, with a fearless vulnerability. These simple truths will inspire you to experience God the Father, Jesus, and the Holy Spirit in an intimate manner. Open this book and open your heart!

-Andrea Anderson LPC, NCC, MA
Clinical Psychotherapist
www.andreaandersonlpc.com

I have had the wonderful opportunity to minister with Rachel Godfrey and see firsthand some of the miracles God has performed through her. Rachel is the real deal, as you will experience for yourself in *"From A Heart of Stone."* If you have ever questioned the "how to's" of life in the spirit or wondered as you listened to someone else's encounter of the miracle realm, then this book is for you! Rachel speaks candidly about her Christian walk through her relationship with the Holy Spirit, explaining and instructing so perfectly her first encounters with the Spirit of God. She teaches through her gift of humor and wit. I was drawn in immediately, as you will be also!

-Leslie Tracey
Cofounder/President, Double Portions Ministries
www.dpministries.net

Empowering, revelatory, and LIFE CHANGING!! Reading *"From a Heart of Stone"* will leave you hungering for deep relationship with Holy Spirit. The powerful anointing on this book will set you free!

-Iris Stephens
Physical Therapist Assistant, Evangelist

Rachel writes as if she personally knows Holy Spirit. This is because she does! Rachel's warm and compassionate stories of her encounters with the Holy Spirit of God will both encourage and edify the reader. Rachel helps instruct and guide the student into their own grand adventure, pointing them to Jesus. A greatly inspiring book! Bravo!

-Edie Bayer
Author of *"Power Thieves: 7 Spirits That Steal Your Power* and *How to Get it Back!*
Edie@KingdomPromoters.org
www.KingdomPromoters.org

Get ready for an eye-opening, ear opening, Spirit filled adventure into the transformational encounter that only the Holy Spirit can do. Rachel guides you through the many ways you may encounter the Holy Spirit and how He can speak. She opens her life so that you may learn and know with assurance the Holy Spirit is also speaking to you. This book is for old, young, and seasoned Christians and those who may have not realized there is a God who is speaking to them. You are led through teaching of the Word that drops you into present day reality encounters. Not only does Rachel reveal her heart to you, but you are activated into your own adventure with your friend the Holy Spirit.

-Christy Race
Physical Therapist/Author of the children's book *"The Gift"*

More than ever, our generation is longing to see Jesus as the relevant, personal and living God that He is through the Holy Spirit. Rachel beautifully combines her own modern-day stories of God's amazing work with the powerful timeless stories of the Bible. This book will leave you touched by God's present-day love and miracles as well as hungry to see Him revealed in your own life and in this generation.

-Michelle P.
Overseas Worker

"From a Heart of Stone" is a book for our time. Rachel Godfrey draws us into her life of encounters with the Holy Spirit so that experiencing the Holy Spirit becomes the norm instead of the exception, and clearly shows us how to not only hear His voice, but experience His operation in our lives, as well. We laughed and we cried as we read her stories. This is a message new Christians need to hear. This is a message not-on-fire Christians need to get! Walking with the Holy Spirit as Rachel describes will take us through the end-times and prepare us with the fragrance to meet Jesus

-Mike & Cindy Teagarden
Founders, Deep Water Ministries Int'l
www.deepwaterhealing.com

Table of Contents

Acknowledgments

My life is a testimony of the faithfulness of Father God, Jesus Christ, His Son, and the Holy Spirit AND Their redeeming love. They receive all of my gratitude and appreciation for what They have put into me and brought from within me.

I would also like to thank the two most amazing parents a person could ever have - Dennis and Nancy Godfrey - for the unconditional love and support they have always given me and for placing within me a desire and an ability to work towards my dreams, knowing and believing that they can and will ALL come true. There will never be enough words to express how grateful I am to you and for how much I love you! Thanks Mom and Dad!!

Of course, I must take time to thank the leadership of my home church, Living Faith Church in Manassas, Virginia. Pastor Barry Lubbe for your love of the gospel and your ability to make the scriptures come alive for us in today's world, for following the call that God has on your life, and for being an amazing father of our house. Pastor Joan Lubbe for encouraging me and pouring your heart and your love into me; especially back when I was filled with so much confusion and pain in those early days. Pastor Bill Hajtun for recognizing my gift for writing and encouraging me to find out what exactly Holy Spirit wanted me to do with it. Pastor JR Judd, Pastor Gavin Lubbe, and Pastor David Hajtun for always making me feel special and loved and for showing me what a godly man should look like. Pastor Bebette Hensley-Williams for showing me what it looks like to take God out of the box and allow Him to be God and for creating such a desire in me to really know who the Holy Spirit is. And Pastor Cathy Morris for loving me right where I am, seeing me for who I am and not allowing me to settle for anything less than who God created me to be, and for opening my eyes to what an experience with Holy Spirit could actually look like!

I would also like to thank Sally Tomko, Pastor Joan, Pastor Bebette, and Pastor Cathy (all from Living Faith Church) for working so diligently with me and "my issues" and for bringing me into a freedom I have never experienced before. Thank you for showing me the kind of life that I was meant to live, and for continually encouraging me when life sometimes felt too hard.

I want to thank my instructors in the Living Faith Ministry Training Center (LFMTC). Pastor Barry (Father of the house), Pastor Cathy (Dean of the MTC), Pastor Joan (Mother of the House), Pastor Bebette, Pastor

JR, Pastor Bill, Pastor Sean, Terry Arnone, Heather Craig, Grace Yum, Phyllis Judd, Carol Flack, and Rita Rodgers for pouring your hearts out, opening my eyes to some of the deeper beauties of the Gospel, and for creating in me an insatiable desire to know and to have a relationship with Father God, His Son Jesus Christ, and the Holy Spirit. It was your love, knowledge, teaching, and experience that brought this book into existence - you just didn't know it! (or maybe you did)!

I would also like to give a shout of thanks to my dear friends and mentors, Ann Thornsbury and Missy Dubyak. You have taken me under your wings, mentored me, encouraged me, and loved me as a fellow nurse, as a friend, and as a sister. I treasure you!

A special thank you must also be given to my friend and classmate Andrea Anderson for continuously telling me AND speaking over me that I had something important to say and that I needed to share what Holy Spirit had placed in my heart. Your constant encouragement to be bold and to begin writing helped lay the foundation for this book's existence. My love and gratitude to you, my dear friend and sister.

I would also like to thank Pastor Jeff Marton and his wife April from the H.O.P.E. Center in Belle Vernon, Pennsylvania for pastoring me in those early years of my Christian walk before I found a church home in Virginia. It was your friendship and love that helped to clear some of the confusion and frustration I was feeling in the early years of my Christian walk.

Speaking of those early years, they would not have existed without the love and perseverance of my friends Bethanie, Michelle, Maria, Elizabeth, Deborah, Erin, and Paige. You loved me right into a relationship with Jesus! You will NEVER truly know or understand how much your love, friendship, and sisterhood have meant to me over the years. Without you ladies, this book would NEVER have existed.

A big shout out to Joan Hunter Murrell and her husband Kelly Murrell of Joan Hunter Ministries for loving me from day one, believing in me, guiding me, and for the constant encouragement (and example) to live my life filled with the power of the Holy Spirit. You hold a very special place in my life and in my heart.

I'm also grateful for the mentorship, guidance, prayers, and love that I have received over the years from Mike and Cindy Teagarden of Deep Water Ministries International and Don and Christine Gallagan of FireStorm Street Evangelism. Your example, your love, and your friendship helped to break down some very tough walls around my heart. Long live the Philippines!

And I cannot forget my inner circle, the 5 AMAZING women God has so graciously put into my life - Iris Stephens, Christy Race, Courtney Bowers-Artiste, Barbara Rucci, and Leslie Tracey. We met in Haiti on a missions trip with Joan Hunter Ministries and have been connected ever since. You pray with me and for me, advise me and encourage me, check on me, and love me right where I am, without judgment - weaknesses and all! God knew when He was creating me in my mother's womb, how important you would be to me in my life and I can't imagine going forward without you. Thank you all for being Godly examples of women in strong relationships with Holy Spirit! I have learned so much from you!

Finally, I would like to give a special shout out to Courtney Bowers-Artiste of TNT Publishing for walking through every step of this journey with me, for encouraging me, tolerating me, but most importantly for being a special sister and friend. My life would NEVER be the same without you in it! And I know for sure that I probably wouldn't be a published author today if it had not been for your encouragement that I COULD write a book and I WOULD (and did) write it well.

This particular section of the book was the second most difficult part for me to write. I put it off until the very end for fear that I might forget to mention or thank someone who is especially important to me and/or to the coming forth of this book. Then it would go to print and my unintentional blunder would forever be in print. So, with that said, in mentioning just a few of you, I am really thanking you all because so many of you have encouraged me along the way. I'm pretty sure that I would never have completed this book without all of you. Thank you is never enough, but it's what I have! Love to all of you!

Foreword

What a privilege to have been asked by Rachel to write the foreword for her very first book. Having known her for many years now, I am able to say that she is one of the most pure hearted individuals that I am acquainted with. Her earnest desire to know God in a deeper and deeper fashion and then to share Him with others is quite captivating. She is very determined to "freely give what she has freely received".

I met Rachel when she came to our church and applied for admission to our Ministry Training Center. She was very excited and extremely curious about the things of God and about growing proficient in the "abundant life" that Jesus spoke of. As I watched her in her studies, I could see that she was completely committed to her relationship with the Father. It was also evident early on that she was very diligent and teachable in every area of her life. She took her learning experience seriously and was not willing to allow anything to stand in her way. As the years passed, I saw her grow and mature and blossom in the beautiful freedom that comes only by the Holy Spirit. After completing four years of school, she graduated and then set out to explore further. She began to pursue any opportunity she could find to benefit others with the truth that she had learned. I have seen her work very hard all week at her job and then spend her weekends ministering to others. Not only that, but she often uses her vacation time for mission trips. This is the lady that is inviting you to step with her through a door of endless possibilities as you develop deeper fellowship with the Spirit.

As you begin reading this book, I would encourage you to open up and trust Father God to plant some very hybrid seed in the center of your heart. He would just love to stimulate a hunger within you that can only be satisfied by a very rich and fulfilling relationship with Him. Rachel has this radical hunger. I know because I have watched her seek and seek to her hearts' content. She is the right person to guide you into an adventure of a lifetime... a journey on a beautiful path that leads directly into the center of many experiences that Father God has specifically designed just for you. Feel safe and free to explore the truth of God in a fresh new way. I believe no matter how many people read this book, each of them will receive differently. That's just the way our heavenly Father is – He shares with each of us in such a very personal fashion. Enjoy!

Cathy Morris
Pastor and Director
Living Faith Ministry Training Center

Preface

If I could implore you to take a moment to quiet yourself and just imagine that you have been given the opportunity to have a sit-down, in-person chat with the Holy Spirit. Picture a time, without limits, to focus on developing a true relationship with Him just like you would develop a relationship with anyone else. This will become a time that is so unforgettable, a time that fills you with joy, happiness, peace, and love; a time that you cannot explain away, nor can you truly comprehend what you are experiencing.

What would you ask Him? What do you think He would tell you? How would you feel? What would you want to know?

The truth is, because of Jesus' victory on the cross AND His resurrection by the power of the Holy Spirit, you CAN ask Him all of these questions and so much more! Why? Because He wants to be in a relationship with you, even more than you want to be in a relationship with Him. You CAN experience the most amazing, loving, faithful Person to EVER exist. There's just one catch: you have to be willing to step out in faith, get rid of your "religious" ideas of Who He is, and allow yourself to encounter the most amazing Person you will EVER have the honor and privilege to meet.

That's what you're about to read in this book. I want to show you how amazing and wonderful He is by sharing a small glimpse of my experiences with the Holy Spirit. He's a wild, fun Guy! He really is! He's patient, kind, loving, and nurturing - the list could go on and on. That in no way is taking away from the sovereign, Holy God that He is. I just want to show you that He is probably not Who you thought He was. This book is meant to provoke you into finding out for yourself, WHO the Holy Spirit is for you and for goodness sake, to take Him OUT OF THE BOX!

The Holy Spirit is so amazing and that is why I am choosing to dedicate this book to Him! He is the TRUE inspiration behind this book and I am so grateful that these words are more His than mine! He is my BEST friend and He deserves all the honor, glory, power, and so much more! To Him, I owe everything! So, if you are looking for the same kind of relationship that I have with the Holy Spirit, I invite you to quiet yourself, enter into His Presence, and allow Him to take you on the adventure of your life! You life will NEVER be the same. Need a little push? Start reading this book and catch a glimpse of what He has done in MY life!

Introduction

"I will deliver you from the Jewish people, as well as from the Gentiles, to whom I now send you, to open their eyes, in order to turn them from darkness to light, and from the power of satan to God, that they may receive forgiveness of sins and an inheritance among those who are sanctified by faith in Me."
~ Acts 26:17-18

It was a beautiful Sunday morning in September. I had the privilege of attending church with some of my closest friends. It was the first time they had joined me at my home church, Living Faith Church (http://www.livingbyfaith.com) in Manassas, VA. I felt so honored that they were there to worship with me, but having them there left me feeling a little distracted. I struggled to enter into worship with my Lord and Savior because I wanted to make sure their needs were being met.

Finally, I told Holy Spirit that I was sorry that I was not giving Him my entire heart. I wanted Him to understand that I was more cognizant of my friends being there visiting with me and I was continuously thinking about what they might be thinking. Do you know what He told me? *"You don't need to worry about that or them. I AM willing and able to take care of their needs while they are here. I have been doing it all of their lives."* Immediately, I repented, apologized, and entered into worship with my whole heart.

It didn't take long before the Holy Spirit began speaking deeper into my heart. You see, I had been asking Him about the path I should be taking in regards to my writing. He had already spoken to me on many occasions and through many people that I was given a gift for writing and that I needed to start using it for His glory. There were so many ideas swimming around in my heart and in my mind. I knew I just needed to focus on one project at a time, but I had no idea where to start. Today, during worship, the Holy Spirit whispered to my heart, "*I want you to write about your encounters with Me.*" Wow! This was an answer to a question I had asked Him the night before. I just smiled and said, "*Yes, Sir! But I'm not sure there will be enough of them to fill a book...*"

"*That's ok. You just start writing and I will take care of the rest!*" The Holy Spirit said to me.

So, I sat down and began typing away. I could remember five or six encounters at first, which didn't leave me with much of a book, but as I kept typing, more and more encounters began to flood my mind. It was an amazing time with the Holy Spirit, especially since I had believed the lie that I wasn't encountering Him at all! Wow! What a lie, straight from the pit of hell!

Are you aware that when the Holy Spirit brings a lie to your attention and then reveals His truth, healing is almost immediate? It's amazing how your life can change when you focus on the truth! "*And you shall know the truth, and the truth shall set you free.*" (John 8:32) You see, once the lie is revealed and the truth is brought to light, you can no longer be deceived by that lie.

ARE YOU AWARE THAT WHEN THE HOLY SPIRIT BRINGS A LIE TO YOUR ATTENTION AND THEN REVEALS HIS TRUTH, HEALING IS ALMOST IMMEDIATE?

As I sit here tying all of these amazing stories together, Holy Spirit began to take me deeper into what it means to really encounter Him. First, I looked up the definition of the word encounter.

> **Encounter** - to bump into; a meeting with a person or thing, especially a casual, unexpected, or brief meeting;

a meeting of persons or groups that are in conflict or opposition; combat; battle.

Encounters with the Holy Spirit aren't usually planned. They just happen - whenever He wants them to happen. Most times, they are brief, always casual, and only involve conflict when **WE** create the conflict. This is definitely a good description of the encounters I have had with Him. He also told me that anytime there is a dramatic change in a person's life, it is usually because of an encounter with Him. Lives are forever changed. Here are a few examples, (found in the Bible, of course), of people who have encountered the Holy Spirit and had their lives forever changed.

- Enoch, in Genesis 5, began to walk with God at the ripe old age of 65 (see verses 21-23). Scripture tells us that he walked with God for 300 years.

- Noah (Genesis 6 through 9)

- Abraham had MANY encounters (Genesis 12:1-7; 13:14-17; 15:1-20; 17:1-22; 22:1-19)

- Even Hagar (Sarah's maidservant) had an encounter (Gen 16:7-13)

- Isaac had encounters with God (Genesis 22:1-19)

- Jacob (Genesis 28:10-22; 32:22-32; 35:1-3, 9-15)

- Joseph (Genesis 37:5-9; 40; 41)

- Moses (Book of Exodus)

- Mary (Luke 1:26-38)

- Saul of Tarsus, who became Paul (Acts 9)

Trust me! This is an EXTREMELY short list, but I think it's enough to give you a good idea of how someone MAY encounter the Holy Spirit and how their lives were changed because of it!

However, there is one encounter found in the book of Isaiah that really caught my attention. It's found in the sixth chapter, and starts with the first verse.

> **1** *In the year that King Uzziah died, I saw the Lord sitting on a throne, high and lifted up, and the train of His robe filled the temple.* **2** *Above it stood seraphim; each one had six wings: with two he covered his face, with two he covered his feet, and with two he flew.* **3** *And one cried to another and said: "Holy, holy, holy is the LORD of hosts; The whole earth is full of His glory!"* **4** *And the posts of the door were shaken by the voice of him who cried out, and the house was filled with smoke.* **5** *So I said: "Woe is me, for I am undone! Because I am a man of unclean lips, And I dwell in the midst of a people of unclean lips; For my eyes have seen the King, The LORD of hosts."* **6** *Then one of the seraphim flew to me, having in his hand a live coal which he had taken with the tongs from the altar.* **7** *And he touched my mouth with it, and said: "Behold, this has touched your lips; Your iniquity is taken away, And your sin purged."* **8** *Also I heard the voice of the Lord, saying: "Whom shall I send, And who will go for Us?" Then I said, "Here am I! Send me."* **9** *And He said, "Go, and tell this people: 'Keep on hearing, but do not understand; Keep on seeing, but do not perceive.'* **10** *"Make the heart of this people dull, And their ears heavy, And shut their eyes; Lest they see with their eyes, And hear with their ears, And understand with their heart, And return and be healed."* **11** *Then I said, "Lord, how long?" And He answered: "Until the cities are laid waste and without inhabitant, The houses are without a man, The land is utterly desolate,* **12** *The LORD has removed men far away, And the forsaken places are many in the midst of the land.* **13** *But yet a tenth will be in it, And will return*

and be for consuming, As a terebinth tree or as an oak, Whose stump remains when it is cut down. So the holy seed shall be its stump." ~ Isaiah 6:1-13

You see, Isaiah was just going about his normal day. Every day, he went to the temple to pray, to meditate, and study the scriptures. On this **one** particular day, the roof came off the temple and he could see the Lord sitting on the throne. He didn't do anything different from the day before. Imagine if he would have decided to sleep in that day or to change his routine...

This is what I bring to you in the pages of this book. MY encounters with the Holy Spirit. It is my hope that it will encourage you to seek out your very own encounters with Him.

Before I share my encounters with you, I thought it might be helpful to introduce you to The Holy Spirit.

Who IS this HOLY SPIRIT?

First and foremost, Holy Spirit is a member of the Godhead. Just look at Matthew 28:19 and you will notice how Jesus, who is speaking in this scripture, puts the Holy Spirit on the same level as the Father and the Son with the same authority, power, and glory (See also Acts 5:3-4). He has all the same attributes of God.

- Eternal (see Hebrews 9:14)

- Omnipresent (see Psalm 139:7-8) - He is Everywhere

- Omnipotent (see Luke 1:35) -- He has ALL power

- Omniscient (see 1 Corinthians 2:10) -- He knows ALL things

- Majestic, Holy, & Glorious, too!

The next thing to realize about the Holy Spirit is that He has a personality. He is a person. I mean, how else would He be able to understand us if He didn't have a personality too? Neither stones, trees, nor water can have a conversation with us, but the Holy Spirit sure can.

Need proof? In the Bible, the Holy Spirit is referred to using personal pronouns (See John 15:26; 16:7-8, 13). The word "He" is assigned attributes that only a "person" could have. Check out these documented characteristics below:

- He speaks (Revelation 2:7)

- He prays for us (Romans 8:26)

- He comforts (Acts 9:31)

- He guides (John 16:13)

- He testifies of the Lord (John 15:26)

- He calls people to the work of God (Acts 13:2)

- He commands people (Acts 16:6-7)

- He teaches (John 14:26)

- He has knowledge (mind) (1 Corinthians 2:10; Romans 8:27)

- He has emotions and feelings (Romans 5:5; Ephesians 4:30; Romans 8:26)

- He has a will (1 Corinthians 2:11; Acts 16:6-7)

We need to realize that Holy Spirit is someone who loves and cares for us. He is NOT a bundle of warm feelings and memories, nor is He a vague cosmic force. He is a person who has a mind, will, and emotions and He lives inside of every believer (1 Corinthians 4:4).

Think about Him this way. Jesus was God to the disciples. Holy Spirit is God for us today! Jesus promised to leave us another helper (John 14:16-17) and that helper is the Holy Spirit. Call on Him now to open your spiritual eyes (Ephesians 1:17-19) as you read this book and allow Him to touch your heart and mind and bring about change that only He can.

JESUS PROMISED TO LEAVE US ANOTHER HELPER AND THAT HELPER IS THE HOLY SPIRIT.

Chapter One

Returning to Jesus

"For God so loved the world, that He gave His only Begotten Son, so that whoever believed in Him should not perish but have everlasting life." ~ John 3:16

This story has to begin with my very first, recognizable encounter with the Holy Spirit. I say "recognizable" because I do believe that He has ALWAYS been speaking to me and encountering me, but I didn't recognize it – mainly because of ignorance or sometimes even by choice. Once I CHOSE to accept Him as my Lord and Savior, the journey to encounter Him began.

It started when I read the book, "*When God Writes Your Love Story*" by Eric and Leslie Ludy. At the time, I was a non-practicing Mormon, but my life was a mess and I needed Jesus more than ever. At the end of the book, there was a prayer that I read, inviting Jesus into my heart. Within two weeks, I hit rock bottom. One would think that your life would get better when you invite Jesus into your heart, but alas, that is not usually the case. Anyway, I don't believe I could have gone any lower. I'm sure that you are wondering where in the world this story is going. Somewhere beautiful, I promise.

Not long after hitting rock bottom, the Lord brought an amazing woman named Bethanie into my life. We worked together as ER nurses at the local hospital on the night shift and quickly became friends. We talked about everything and anything, including religion. Bethanie was (and still is) a Christian. Amazing thing to me is I thought I was a Christian, too. I mean, Jesus Christ WAS in the name of the Church, "The Church of Jesus Christ of Latter-day Saints!" Unfortunately, I couldn't have been more wrong. Thankfully, I have a Savior Who loved me even when I was deceived. He brought amazing people into my life to guide me back to Him.

Bethanie loved me where I was, and that my friends, was not an easy job for her. I was a bitter, angry woman. Yet, she loved me anyway. I was short tempered, foul-mouthed, and generally just ugly. She loved me anyway. It was so bad at times; she took it upon herself to protect me from my coworkers, unbeknownst to me. I was not an easy project, yet she did it anyway. However, she was never alone.

First of all, she enlisted the help of her family, her friends, and her church. For three solid years, they ALL prayed for me to encounter Jesus. Throughout that time, Bethanie never stopped loving me and Jesus never stopped pursuing me.

Three years of prayers were finally about to be answered. Brian, Bethanie's husband, asked her to marry him and she, of course, said, "Yes!" Through this wedding, I had the pleasure and privilege of meeting a lot of her friends and family who, unbeknownst to me, had been praying for me all along. They, too, began loving on me and accepting me right where I was - a Mormon girl who didn't know she wasn't a Christian.

Two of Bethanie's friends, Michelle and Maria, took a particular interest in me and began building friendships with me. Michelle would call and leave messages telling me that Jesus loved me and that He had exactly what I was looking for, or she would leave me a voicemail, sharing what Jesus had told her to tell me on that particular day. Maria and I shared many Skype phone calls from her missionary post in South Korea, answering any and every question that I had. Then it happened...

During one of our Skype chats, Maria made a statement that changed my life forever. She said, "*You know Rachel, the truth, twisted just a little bit, is no longer truth.*" Then I knew. I had

...THE TRUTH, TWISTED JUST A LITTLE BIT, IS NO LONGER TRUTH.

been deceived. The Latter-day Saints (aka Mormons) used a lot of the same terminology, but they do NOT believe in the same Jesus as the Christian church does. Do the research, study the Bible, study your heart, and get with God. He is the Author of all truth, in fact, He IS truth - and the truth will set you free! (John 8:32)

After hearing Maria's statement, I immediately dropped to my knees and asked her what I needed to do. She made some suggestions, which unlocked the door to amazing encounters with Jesus. He pursued me and pursued me until my spirit could no longer deny that the Son of God was chasing me and desired to make me His! At that time, I didn't really understand all of that. But over the years, as I grow with Him, He continues to show me how much He loves me, how much He thinks about me, and how much He cherishes me.

Some of you may be asking how I could classify that as an encounter with the Holy Spirit. Well, let me tell you, when the Creator of this world touches your heart, you know it and you will never be the same. The Holy Spirit met me there in the wee hours of the morning and started me on a journey that has brought me to today and will continue to lead me to where God is taking me tomorrow.

Saul of Tarsus (later known as Paul) had an even more amazing encounter with the Holy Spirit than I did. His encounter was so life changing that the Holy Spirit changed his name from Saul to Paul! (see Acts 9:1-20 for the story)

Saul's story is one of the most dramatic accounts of repentance in the entire Bible. He originated from Tarsus and made his way to Jerusalem to study the Law of Moses. Saul LOVED the Law of Moses and despised anyone who didn't. So much so, that he made it his life's mission to remove those followers of Jesus that were making a mockery out of it. He was so good at torturing and traumatizing the believers of Jesus, that most of them fled and/or hid whenever they heard he was anywhere in the vicinity.

Saul and a group of his friends were traveling north of Jerusalem on their way to Damascus when all of a sudden, a great light shone from the sky and Saul fell to the ground. His friends thought they heard thunder, but Saul actually heard the voice of the Lord saying,

"Saul, Saul! Why are you persecuting me?" ~ Acts 9:4

Saul was both amazed and terrified. All of this time, he had thought he was protecting the true religion when he opposed those who believed in Jesus.

He cried out, "*Who are you, Lord?*" Jesus replied, "*I am Jesus of Nazareth, whom you are persecuting.*" (verse 5) I can only imagine that Saul instantly remembered how awful he had treated the men who believed in this Jesus. How wrong he had been! When he asked, "*What shall I do, Lord?*" Jesus told him, "*Get up and go into Damascus. There you will be told what you must do.*" (verse 6)

There was no hesitation on Saul's part. He got up immediately. However, the great light had blinded his eyes. The men who were with Saul had not been blinded, so they led Saul, trembling with fright, into the city, to the house of Judas.

Three days passed, and still Saul could not see. He sat alone in his darkness. I can only imagine how, in his heart, he must have been so disturbed, as evidenced by his inability or desire to eat or drink (verse 9). He had been so wrong!

How many of you think this was a life-changing encounter with the Holy Spirit? It was so life changing that Saul became reborn as Paul, who was chosen by the Lord to be his representative, His apostle, and the primary writer of the New Testament. He no longer had a desire to torture or kill the followers of Jesus and had now become one of them because of this amazing unexpected encounter.

Now, you must realize that most encounters are not always THAT amazing, but they ARE all supernatural and they are ALL very real. Keep reading to see what amazing things I have had the privilege to experience with the Holy Spirit. Who knows? You may just change your definition of the word amazing! If you have never had the opportunity to accept Jesus as your Lord and Savior, please see *Appendix A* and follow the instructions to start your new life with Jesus and the Holy Spirit! Then drop me an email to share about your exciting decision!

Chapter Two

Stakes, Brooms, and Dust, Oh My!

*"I will give you a new heart and put a new spirit in you;
I will remove from you your heart of stone and give you
a heart of flesh." ~ Ezekiel 36:26*

Encountering the Holy Spirit for the first time was absolutely amazing, but there was so much work that needed to be completed in me. Sometimes I would get so discouraged as I continued to make the same mistakes over and over, and it seemed like nothing would EVER change. Thankfully, God promised in Ezekiel 36:26 (see above) that there wasn't a thing we have to do. He would remove the *heart of stone* and replace it with a softer version, made of flesh.

One of the people I had the pleasure of meeting during Brian and Bethanie's wedding, was Elizabeth. She is a quiet soul with a powerful prayer life, and I consider myself abundantly blessed to include her as one of my inner circle of friends.

Immediately after accepting Jesus as my Lord and Savior, some of my deepest, darkest secrets began to surface. They were ugly! After a couple of months of struggling with this, Bethanie suggested that I head out to Missouri to visit Elizabeth. Elizabeth's parents had a successful prayer ministry and she thought that a week with her and her family might be exactly what I needed. Turns out, she was right!

I had the privilege of spending the week with Elizabeth, getting to know her, and experiencing her love up close and personal. She's a prayer warrior, a wonderful confidant, and an amazing cook. Her love alone could have brought amazing healing to my heart, but Holy Spirit had a much bigger plan for me.

During one of the prayer sessions, Cindy (Elizabeth's mother) was teaching me how to get pictures from God and how to interpret them. This was challenging for me, because I had shut down my imagination a very long time ago. Receiving pictures from God was something I had the hardest time understanding. However, Cindy's skill, persistence, and intimacy with the Holy Spirit, combined with my desire to actually receive these pictures, opened the door for some amazing encounters with the Holy Spirit.

My very first picture has been my favorite so far. It witnessed to me how well Jesus knows me. I don't remember the issue we were dealing with, but I DO remember the picture and what it witnessed to my heart. Now, you have to realize that this is the first picture I had seen using my imagination, probably since childhood. It took Cindy's masterful skill and gentle encouragement to help develop this picture, because I definitely wasn't trusting what I was seeing.

She kept asking me, "*What's going on, Rachel? What do you see or what are you seeing?*" It took me a while to acknowledge that I was actually seeing something. Finally, I decided to take a chance and try to explain what I thought I was seeing. You could say I chose to step out in faith and believe that what I was seeing in my mind was indeed from God. What I saw was a human heart - a real, live, beating heart. It wasn't connected to any body. It was just there in the middle of my "screen". What made this picture so unique for me were the 20+ wooden spikes going all the way through the heart in all different directions.

After I hesitantly described what I was seeing, Cindy asked me what I thought it meant. I didn't have a clue. It was overwhelming enough to see the picture, let alone try to figure out what it could possibly mean. I wasn't even convinced that I was actually seeing anything.

A few minutes later she said, "*Let's ask Holy Spirit what it means.*" Sounds simple right? Not so much! My analytical mind was struggling to wrap itself around this experience, but I had nothing to lose, so I asked Holy Spirit, "*What does this picture mean?*" He responded almost immediately, "*Pull one of those stakes out and give it to Me. It doesn't matter which one.*" There was NO WAY I was going to do that. The nurse in me KNEW that if I pulled one of those stakes out, it would leave a gaping hole in that human heart. All the blood would come squirting out, and the heart would die. Somehow, I knew that I did NOT want that heart to die.

Isn't it interesting how invested I became in this vision that just a few minutes before, I wasn't even convinced was real? Well, all of a sudden, I was unable to separate reality from this vision. I became emotionally invested in what happened to this heart - which, by the way, could never function on its own, outside of the body, but at that moment, that was not relevant. In this picture, I did not want to pull that stake out under ANY circumstances.

We went round and round for a good 15 minutes or so. Holy Spirit gently asking me to remove one of the stakes and me arguing that if I did, the heart would die. Stubbornly, I decided to go ahead and pull out that stake - just to prove that I was right. Wow! The audacity of that thought still amazes me today. Really? I'm going to show the Creator of the universe and beyond that He was wrong! Seriously? So, I reached out and pulled the stake out, expecting blood to come gushing out of the open wound, but guess what? That is NOT what happened! As soon as I pulled that stake out, the heart muscle sealed itself, perfectly. Not one drop of blood escaped from the heart! Not one! Now, who was proving something to whom?

Normally, you might think that the next stake would have been easier to remove, but alas, it was not. Removing the first stake from the heart was so unbelievable that I could not believe that it could or would, happen again. Here was Holy Spirit, asking me to remove another stake, and there I was, refusing to pull that stake out AGAIN. I am so grateful that Holy Spirit is so patient, so kind, and so understanding. He was not in a rush at all. He was teaching me to trust Him. Eventually, in less time than it took for the first stake, I reached up and pulled out the second stake and the same thing happened - the heart immediately sealed over the hole left by that stake, almost before the stake had been completely removed. This was really becoming fun! I pulled out every single stake in that heart, and every single time, the heart was immediately healed and made completely whole.

As challenging as I found it to pull out those stakes, His next request was even harder. Holy Spirit asked me to give Him the stakes. For a reason I cannot explain, I could not give Him those stakes. My mind could not give Holy Spirit a logical explanation except that I just didn't want to give them to Him.

How foolish of me! Holy Spirit was showing me that there were many wounds throughout my heart. Each one caused by those stakes. He revealed the cause of those wounds and showed me how He would heal them! Even with all of that, I still struggled to trust Him with those things that were most painful to me. Thankfully, Cindy is gifted with patience, understanding, and wisdom, too! She was able to walk through this entire vision with me and eventually, I was able to hand over ALL of those stakes to Holy Spirit.

The funny thing is, at the time, I didn't really feel any different. I didn't feel free like I was expecting to feel, but that didn't matter. Almost ten years later, He is STILL teaching me about that first vision, and I can promise you that I am walking in a greater freedom than I have ever known!

A session or two later, I encountered Holy Spirit once again through another vision. Two visions in a matter of days and I couldn't even remember the last time I had even used my imagination.

The second vision was just as much of a struggle as the first one. We were talking about anger and I would not or maybe could not admit that I was a VERY angry woman. The anger had become so much a part of me that I didn't even recognize it for what it was. Thankfully, though, I have a Friend (Holy Spirit) who didn't want me to hold onto that anger any longer.

Anyway, we were talking about anger and I was actively denying that I had any. Cindy suggested I picture this "non-existent" anger sprinkled all over the floor like dust. It took some time, but eventually I was able see it. Once I saw it, she asked me to take a broom and sweep up that anger into a big pile and to let her know when I was finished. Fifteen minutes later, I still had not told her that I was finished. So, Cindy asked me what was going on. I told her that I was still sweeping. Can you believe that? Another 15 minutes went by before I had it all in a big pile and told her I was finished. She just smiled at me and said, "*That sure was a lot of sweeping for a woman who didn't have any anger.*" I replied, "*I know! Right?*"

She then had me ask Holy Spirit what He wanted me to do with that pile and He said, "*Give it to me.*" Now, I consider myself a smart girl, but I again struggled with giving Him that pile of anger. Fortunately, though, I did not take as long as I had the day before.

Finally, I swept the anger into a number of garbage bags and willingly gave them to Him. When I did, I felt a release. I can't really explain it, except, the heaviness that had been resting on my shoulders for my entire adult life was gone. It had been there for so long that it had become part of me. So much so, that when it was gone, it was noticeable, almost palpable. It felt like 30 pounds had been taken off my shoulders. After giving Holy Spirit all of that anger, combined with all of those stakes from the day before, I was starting to FEEL the difference! Having this encounter with the Holy Spirit made a HUGE difference in my life and I KNOW it WILL make a difference in your life, too!

Some of you reading this may feel a little uncomfortable with what I just shared. I want you to know that I was EXTREMELY uncomfortable when it was happening to me. This was an entirely new experience for me and my analytical mind was not sure how to process it or what to do with it. The wonderful thing is, I didn't need to understand what was taking place to receive my healing or my freedom. I just had to receive. As Holy Spirit continues to shape and mold me over the years, He has shown me that He indeed does communicate with us through pictures and visions that He brings to our SPIRITUAL eyes.

Did you know that the Bible shows us how we should be seeing through our spiritual eyes? Well, it does. Take a look at this:

> "*17* that the God of our Lord Jesus Christ, the Father of glory, may give to you the spirit of wisdom and revelation in the knowledge of Him, *18* the eyes of your understanding being enlightened; that you may know what is the hope of His calling, what are the riches of the glory of His inheritance in the saints, *19* and what is the exceeding greatness of His power toward us who believe, according to the working of His mighty power"
> ~ Ephesians 1:17-19

If Paul believed it (seeing in the Spirit, visions, etc.) was only available to a chosen few, why would he have prayed for everyone to receive it?

Now take a look at this.

> "*15* And when the servant of the man of God arose early and went out, there was an army, surrounding the city with horses and chariots. And his servant said to him, "Alas, my master! What shall we do?" *16* So he answered, "Do not fear, for those who are with us are more than those who are with them." *17* And Elisha prayed, and said, "LORD, I pray, open his eyes that he may see." Then the LORD opened the eyes of the young man, and he saw.

> *And behold, the mountain was full of horses and chariots of fire all around Elisha." ~* 2 Kings 6:15-17

Did you notice that Elisha didn't pray, "*Lord, if it be my servant's gifting, open his eyes*," He asked the Lord to open his servant's eyes, and guess what? The Lord opened his servant's spiritual eyes to see in the spiritual realm.

Now, here's how it becomes relevant for today. God is the same today, tomorrow, and forever (Hebrews 13:8) AND, He is no respecter of persons (Acts 10:34). If He opened the spiritual eyesight of Elisha's servant, it serves to reason that He would do the same thing for us. Besides, God is God, and He is AMAZING. He can choose to teach us and communicate with us in any way He chooses. So, why not visions?

Check out this revelation in Revelations 3:18!

> **18** *"Here's what I want you to do: Buy your gold from me, gold that's been through the refiner's fire. Then you'll be rich. Buy your clothes from me, clothes designed in Heaven. You've gone around half-naked long enough.* ***And buy medicine for your eyes from me so you can see, really see.***" (emphasis added)

GOD WANTS TO ANOINT OUR EYES WITH SPIRITUAL EYE SALVE SO WE CAN SEE INTO THE SPIRIT REALM.

God wants to anoint our eyes with spiritual eye salve so we can see into the spirit realm. This promise is for EVERY believer, not just a few. I am a believer and I claim and receive this amazing promise. The exciting thing about this is He gave it to me before I even knew it was mine to receive. Why? Because MY God is incredible, amazing, and full of love because He is Love (1 John 4:8).

What about Luke 4:18?

> *"The Spirit of the* LORD *is upon Me, Because He has anointed Me to preach the gospel to the poor; He has sent Me to heal the brokenhearted, To proclaim liberty to the captives And recovery of sight to the blind, To set at liberty those who are oppressed;"*

Most people don't associate this verse with spiritual blindness and/or sight, but what if it was? Think about it from this angle. Jesus started by saying he was anointed to preach the gospel to the poor - spiritual activity, right? He also talks about bringing freedom to prisoners and those who are oppressed. Does it say anywhere in scripture that Jesus went around releasing people from prison while He ministered on the earth? No, it doesn't. He healed hearts and freed many who were oppressed by the devil. None of those things are really seen in the physical body. Therefore, I conclude that the "*recovery of the sight to the blind*" is not just limited to healing the physically blind, but the spiritually blind, as well.

Then what about the verses that talk about having a plank in your eye and your brother's eye?

> *1 "Judge not, that you be not judged. 2 For with what judgment you judge, you will be judged; and with the measure you use, it will be measured back to you. 3 And why do you look at the speck in your brother's eye, but do not consider the plank in your own eye? 4 Or how can you say to your brother, 'Let me remove the speck from your eye'; and look, a plank is in your own eye? 5 Hypocrite! First remove the plank from your own eye, and then you will see clearly to remove the speck from your brother's eye. ~ Matthew 7:1-5*

You and I both know that Jesus is not speaking about the physical eye. He is telling us how we see our world through the eyes of our heart and how that PLANK prevents us from seeing into the spiritual realm.

To finish out this chapter, I want to ask you a question. If we hate or despise another person, do we go physically blind? If you read 1 John 2:11 and took it literally, you might think that. Take a look.

> *"But he who hates his brother is in darkness and walks in darkness, and does not know where he is going, because the darkness has blinded his eyes."*

What I'm trying to get across to you right now is that we have physical eyesight and we have spiritual eyesight. God can choose to communicate with us using either one, but because He is Spirit (John 4:24), He chooses to communicate with our spirits. Hate and unforgiveness obscures our view and destroys our discernment. Therefore, preventing us from seeing with our spiritual eyes as much as we could be.

I don't know about you, but I want to have everything Jesus died on the cross to give me. So, if He chooses to give me visions to understand Him better or to understand what is hindering me from living the life He promised (John 10:10), I will be chasing after those visions until He takes me home.

So, what are you seeing?

Chapter Three

Miracles in Narnia

"*Therefore He who supplies the Spirit to you and works miracles among you, does He do it by the works of the law, or by the hearing of faith?*" ~ *Galatians 3:5*

In 2006, I had the tremendous privilege of visiting my friend, Michelle, while she served as a missionary in Narnia. (The name of the country is not disclosed for her safety). It was my first night in the country. I had traveled over 20 hours to get there and had been awake about 36 hours or so. We had finally arrived at her humble little home and I could feel the exhaustion from the trip and lack of sleep, overtaking my body. However, Michelle wanted to make me a nice dinner to celebrate my arrival. How could I refuse?

I offered to help, of course, but Michelle would have no part of that. She just wanted me to rest, as she prepared a meal of chicken curry and rice (over a Bunsen burner, I might add) with a salad. As she began her preparations, her entranceway became crowded with 10-12 neighboring children who were all clamoring about to meet Michelle's "sister" who had come from a faraway place. They were pushing and shoving each other, trying to get a good look at me, when Michelle took a moment to speak to them in a soft, quiet, but stern voice and everyone settled down. She turned around, smiled, and said, "*They just want to help me make dinner for you!*"

That really warmed my heart! I could feel the exhaustion overtaking me, so I sat back with wonder and watched how they all washed their hands, helped to cut up the chicken, cook the rice, and even cut up the salad. As the preparations were being made with so much love, Michelle realized that the children would expect to be able to partake of the meal and she knew that she did not have enough to feed so many additional people.

I immediately told her they could have my plate and every plate of food for my entire visit (I had quite a few pounds I could afford to lose). They definitely needed that food a lot more than I did. But, of course, Michelle would not have any of that either. I asked her if we could just pray over the food and see what God was going to do. Yep, this was me, asking Michelle to do this. I had NEVER said or done ANYTHING like that before, EVER! Looking back on it now, I don't know where that came from. Of course, I do - it was the Holy Spirit!

As we all sat down around the plate of food, with expectation in our eyes, Michelle prayed over the food, first in English, and then in the local language so the children could understand. Then she handed me a plate of food with utensils, while inviting the children to dig in. NOT ONE of them would eat. In this country, it was customary to eat with your hands. Michelle asked them, *"What's wrong?"*, and they told her they wanted to eat like her, as they pointed at me with my utensils. So, Michelle got forks and spoons for everyone and we all began eating.

Then, the most incredible, amazing thing happened! When we were all finished, there was more food left over than when we started! Yes, you read that correctly! All 15 of us ate until our bellies were full and there was more food left over then when we started! Holy Spirit loved each of us enough, that He multiplied the food so much, there was enough for another meal or two! It was one of the most wonderful meals I had EVER eaten!

Did we notice anything while the meal was being prepared? I don't know about Michelle, but I cannot say that I noticed anything in the natural. However, I do remember just knowing that Holy Spirit was going to step in and provide for us. Had I ever experienced anything like that before? Nope. NEVER!

Where did the faith come from to allow that miracle to happen? I believe I was given one of the gifts of the Holy Spirit - the gift of faith (See 1 Corinthians 12:9). I will remember that encounter for the rest of my life, and I feel so blessed to have been able to participate in a smaller version of Jesus multiplying the food for the four and five thousand (Matthew 14:13-21; Mark 6:30-44; Luke 9:10-17; John 6:1-15; Matthew 15:29-39; Mark 8:1-10).

The other miracle I wanted to share that occurred while I was visiting Michelle in Narnia, happened on a trip we were taking to a small resort town in a nearby country. Michelle had secured taxi transport to get us to the border. We had traveled a good hour before we came to the first police checkpoint, where it was required to show our passports and visas. As I reached into my bag to grab my passport, it wasn't there. Oh my goodness! My heart started racing! I dove into my bag, pushing items around and re-arranging things, trying to find my passport. I couldn't find it anywhere!

The police officer asked us to step out of the car and Michelle began looking through my bag, thinking it was just hidden behind something. She didn't find it either! I couldn't believe this was happening to me! Here I was, in a strange country that speaks a strange language, doesn't like Americans, doesn't respect women, and had a distaste for Christians. Without my passport, I had just ruined our week because now we would probably have to spend the rest of the visit at the US Embassy sorting this entire debacle out, so I could get back to the United States.

I was so disappointed, discouraged, and distressed. The police officer released the taxi to continue on its way and told us he would drive us back to the capital city from where we had come. We walked over to this pile of sand and silently watched as this officer cleaned about 6 inches of sand from a car, (a Yugo) just like I cleaned snow off of my car at home. After the car was cleaned off, we climbed in and started the long, one-hour drive back to the capital city. Michelle kept encouraging me not to worry about it, that we had probably left it on her desk in the office, but I was not so easily convinced.

I looked through my bag for another 15 or 20 minutes without success. Michelle looked again, too. She didn't find it either. My heart was in the pit of my stomach. I could NOT believe it! After traveling all of this way to spend time with Michelle, we were going to be stuck at the embassy without an opportunity to experience her life in Narnia. The disappointment was so palpable. I could feel it getting heavier and heavier, almost to the point of suffocating me.

While we trekked along through the desert in the Yugo, Michelle was having a very animated conversation with the police officer. Every now and then, she would pause to translate for me, but I was so distraught, I didn't catch most of it. She later told me that the police officer had told her that he had read our book, meaning the Bible, and that it had told him that Michelle was to be his wife! Oh my goodness! Seriously? I guess he didn't realize how much she had read "our" book! The conversation continued and I decided to take one more look in my bag, even though I "KNEW" it wasn't going to be there.

As I unzipped the middle compartment of my bag, there it was! There was my passport! I could have leapt right out of the car, had we not been going 70 miles per hour in a Yugo across the desert!

"*Michelle,*" I tried to say in a normal, unexcited tone. "*You're never going to guess what I just found!*"

"*No Way!*" she replied, and we both just began praising God for returning my passport!

The police officer didn't want to be left out, as he jubilantly shouted, "*See? THIS is confirmation that you, referring to Michelle, are meant to be my wife!*" This guy wasn't going to give up so easily!

Thankfully, Michelle had the presence of mind to keep her cool and just laugh it off, which did not please the officer in the least. We arrived back at the taxi yard, in a full 180-degree spin. The car came to a stop and he practically shoved us out, as he sped away in anger because Michelle was not willing to become his wife.

Those were quite the miracles if I DO say so myself!

So what is a miracle? Webster's dictionary defines it as,

> "*An extraordinary event manifesting divine intervention in human affairs; an extremely outstanding or unusual event, thing, or accomplishment.*"

A MIRACLE IS AN EXTRAORDINARY EVENT MANIFESTING DIVINE INTERVENTION IN HUMAN AFFAIRS; AN EXTREMELY OUTSTANDING OR UNUSUAL EVENT, THING, OR ACCOMPLISHMENT.

There are many people who pray for them daily and many more who don't believe that God performs miracles any more. I have a few things to say about that. Let's take a look at the first miracle that Jesus did - the miracle that launched Him into His three-year ministry - where He made wine from water at a wedding He was attending. It is documented in John 2:1-11.

> `1 "On the third day there was a wedding in Cana of Galilee, and the mother of Jesus was there. 2 Now both Jesus and His disciples were invited to the wedding. 3 And when they ran out of wine, the mother of Jesus said to Him, "They have no wine."4 Jesus said to her, "Woman, what does your concern have to do with Me? My hour has not yet come." 5 His mother said to the servants, "Whatever He says to you, do it." 6 Now there were set there six waterpots of stone, according to the manner of purification of the Jews, containing twenty or thirty gallons apiece. 7 Jesus said to them, "Fill the*

waterpots with water." And they filled them up to the brim. **8** *And He said to them, "Draw some out now, and take it to the master of the feast." And they took it.* **9** *When the master of the feast had tasted the water that was made wine, and did not know where it came from (but the servants who had drawn the water knew), the master of the feast called the bridegroom.* **10** *And he said to him, "Every man at the beginning sets out the good wine, and when the guests have well drunk, then the inferior. You have kept the good wine until now!"* **11** *This beginning of signs Jesus did in Cana of Galilee, and manifested His glory; and His disciples believed in Him."*

Verse 11 tells us WHY God uses miracles. Read verse 11 again. This miracle, this sign, this wonder, "manifested His glory AND His disciples believed Him!" THEY BELIEVED HIM. Why did they believe Him? Because Father God produced this miracle through Jesus. So, you see, God uses miracles to help unbelievers believe in Who He is! Think about this. If you saw Jesus turn water into wine, would you not believe in Him, too? I know I definitely would. Of course, some people have trouble believing a man could be raised from the dead.

In the Bible, God shows us how He uses miracles to answer prayers. In Acts 12:1-17, we see how God stepped in and had Peter freed from prison because of the continuous prayers of the church. Let's paint the picture. Peter is arrested, bound with chains, thrown in jail, has a guard on each side of him, and four squads of soldiers outside of his cell. There is no earthly way Peter could have escaped, but God.

An angel of the Lord arrives. Peter's chains fall to the floor. He's instructed to put on his coat and shoes and to follow the angel right out of the jail, past the two guards at his side, past the four squads of soldiers, and out the locked doors through the jail. Even Peter wasn't sure what was happening - he thought he was having a vision and was completely surprised to learn it was all very real.

He heads to a home filled with believers interceding on his behalf. It was such a miracle that even they didn't believe it was him at first. But you can bet this miracle increased their faith in God and in the power of prayer!

How about when God appeared to Moses in the burning bush and called Him to lead the Israelites out of Egypt to the Promised Land? (Exodus 3) He used a miracle, an extraordinary event, to get Moses' attention and to prove that He was God. This miracle was the foundation of Moses' preparation to lead the people of Israel out of the clutches of the Egyptian Pharaoh. Think about it. How would you be affected, if God started talking to you through a bush that appeared to be on fire, yet it wasn't burning? I'm pretty sure most of us would develop faith in God pretty quickly. It's easy to follow God when He's present in a miracle, isn't it?

What about all of the other amazing miracles God performed in front of Pharaoh? There were a LOT of them (See Exodus 7:8-11, 14-21; 8:1-7, 16-17, 20-24; 9:1-6, 8-10, 22-26; 10:12-15, 21-23; 11:29-30). Then God revealed Himself to the world when He divided the Red Sea, allowing the Israelites to walk across dry land and then drowning the Egyptians who tried to follow (Exodus 14).

Let's back up a little further. Abraham and Sarah had a son at the ripe old age of 100. No one believed that Sarah could even get pregnant and when she did, I'm pretty sure most people didn't believe she would carry Isaac to term. Imagine all of their surprise and wonder when Isaac was born to Sarah, who was 90 and Abraham was 100 years old (Genesis 21:1-6).

This miracle solidified the covenant that God made with Abraham that he would be the father of nations (Genesis 13:15-16; 17:1-4) and proved once again, that *"all things are possible with God."* (Matthew 19:26) Miracles are possible because of God (Jeremiah 32:17; Matthew 19:26; Mark 10:27; Luke 1:37). I believe Genesis 2:7 speaks of one of the two greatest miracles known to man.

> *"And the LORD God formed man of the dust of the ground, and breathed into his nostrils the breath of life; and man became a living soul."*

With this miracle, we learn that God is the potter and we are the clay. He can make us or destroy us anytime He chooses. However, I believe He chooses to bring life because not only does it bring Him honor and power, it brings Him great joy and pleasure. Just check out Revelation 4:11 to get a better understanding.

> *"You are worthy, O Lord, To receive glory and honor and power; For You created all things, And by Your will they exist and were created"*

God uses miracles because they bring Him great pleasure. It says it right there!

Ok, so some of you naysayers may say that this proves nothing but the fact that God used or created many miracles throughout the Bible. Think about these three main characteristics of Who God is before you make your final decision.

1. God **cannot** lie (Titus 1:2) - it doesn't say that God WON'T lie; it says He is **unable** to lie.

2. He does not change (Hebrews 13:8) - so, if He does not change, then why would He stop using miracles today when He used them in both the Old and New Testaments?

3. He is no respecter of persons (Acts 10:34) - that tells me He has no "favorites". If God doesn't have any "favorites", then why would He prevent miracles from happening today? If He did it for them, then I would expect Him to do it for us, too. That just tells me that He loves us ALL the same.

Miracles still happen because God STILL wants to show unbelievers Who He is. He still performs miracles because He has a covenant with His children. They happen every day, whether you believe them or not. If He performed a miracle for Peter, Moses, Abraham, Sarah, and for Michelle and me, then He will certainly perform miracles for you. God loves us and He loves doing special things for His children. Paul reminds us of this in Romans 8:38-39.

IF HE PERFORMED A MIRACLE FOR PETER, MOSES, ABRAHAM, SARAH, AND FOR MICHELLE AND ME, THEN HE WILL CERTAINLY PERFORM MIRACLES FOR YOU.

> "**38** For I am persuaded, that neither death, nor life, nor angels, nor principalities, nor powers, nor things present, nor things to come, **39** Nor height, nor depth, nor any other creature, shall be able to separate us from the love of God, which is in Christ Jesus our Lord."

I encourage everyone reading this book to look for the miracles occurring all around you. Ask God to make them plain and clear to you, and you will be blown away at the amazing miracles God is doing every single day!

Chapter Four

Water Baptism

*"When He had been baptized, Jesus came up
immediately from the water; and behold, the heavens
were opened to Him, and He saw the Spirit of God
descending like a dove and alighting upon Him. And
suddenly a voice came from heaven, saying, "This is My
beloved Son, in whom I am well pleased."*
~ Matthew 3:16-17

Ten years prior to the publishing of this book, I recommitted my life to Jesus and wanted to do everything He commanded me to do in the Bible. The most important instruction I remember reading was found in John 14:15, which told me that if I loved Jesus, I would keep His commandments. I pondered that scripture a lot. Did I LOVE Jesus? I wasn't sure. However, I did know I wanted to follow Him and more importantly, I wanted to know Him.

When I was a teenager, I loved learning about Jesus and I loved sharing what I learned with everyone I met. So, you can imagine, the more I learned about Him, the more I wanted to know. Sadly, though, every time I asked about being baptized, I was told I wasn't "ready", although no one could or would tell me what I needed to do, "to be ready". After being told that so many times, I stopped asking. I became so disenchanted with the entire process; I fell away from the church and Jesus. During my college years, I was so easily led astray that I found myself a member of the Church of Jesus Christ of Latter-day Saints just because they were willing to baptize me. Thankfully, fourteen years later, Jesus placed amazing people in my life as I wrote in an earlier chapter, and I was able to commit myself to Him, once again.

Eighteen months after I had accepted Jesus as my Lord and Savior, I was given the amazing opportunity to FINALLY be baptized! My amazing friends (you know who you are) and family came together to help me celebrate this incredible day. They encircled me with love, support, and prayers. Each one made a special effort to join me on that special day as I made my public demonstration that I was, and still am, a disciple of Jesus Christ. I believe that not only was this a confession before man, but it was a confession of faith before the entire kingdom of darkness.

WATER BAPTISM WAS DESIGNED BY GOD AS A PROPHETIC DECLARATION TO THE KINGDOM OF DARKNESS THAT WE BELONG TO A DIFFERENT KING!

You see, I believe water baptism was designed by God as a prophetic declaration to the kingdom of darkness that we belong to a different King!

Do you need to be baptized in order to be saved? I don't believe so. The thief on the cross next to Jesus wasn't baptized, but Jesus promised him that he would be with Him in paradise (Luke 23:43). I believe that Jesus responded to the man's faith and conviction, because there certainly wasn't time for the thief to be baptized before he died on that cross. Salvation comes by faith (Romans 1:16), not by baptism.

However, I do believe that if you're going to start living as an ambassador of the Lord Jesus Christ and His Kingdom, you need to be baptized. Why? Because baptism is a public confession of faith, done in submission to the order of God. It positions us in a place of authority over satan and his demons. There is a very REAL, spiritual dynamic to baptism – it's not just a symbol, as many people believe.

When you are baptized, heaven is opened over you. The Holy Spirit overshadows you. Your eyes and ears are opened to see and hear heavenly realities. The Father affirms you - you are His child. He expresses His approval of you. He tells you He is proud of you. Your identity is now solidified in Christ. You ARE HIS!

WHEN YOU ARE BAPTIZED, HEAVEN IS OPENED OVER YOU. THE HOLY SPIRIT OVERSHADOWS YOU.

Now, when I was baptized, it wasn't done in a church or even affiliated with a church, nor was there a pastor present. What I DID have, was a family who had an exercise pool in their house that the father had added to do strengthening exercises to treat his Multiple Sclerosis. They willingly opened their home and welcomed ALL thirty of us for my baptism. My friend Mark (Maria's husband), who was a missionary, returned from South Korea and baptized me (full immersion) in the name of the Father, the Son, and the Holy Spirit. It was one of the most special days of my life. Each friend or family member present had already made this commitment to Jesus and were there supporting me in love, knowledge, and wisdom. It was amazing!

There are many who believe that baptism is for the church and therefore the church and/or pastor must be present. I have not found that supported anywhere in scripture. I did find John baptizing in the desert (Mark 1:4) and Philip baptizing the Ethiopian by stopping at a pool of water by the side of the road. (Acts 8:36-38) For all we know, it might have even been a puddle left over from the rainy season.

I have even known Christians who question whether baptism is necessary, using the same argument that I used earlier about the man on the cross. We ARE commanded to repent and be baptized (see Acts 2:38) and when someone chooses not to be baptized, they are questioning God's order. Baptism is the second stage in entering the Kingdom of God (only behind accepting Jesus as our Lord and Savior, of course) and submitting to His authority in your life. Think about this. Why wouldn't you want to publicly display your love and obedience to Christ? Are you like the rich man (Mark 10:17-23) who weighed the cost of repentance and decided it wasn't worth the cost, or are you like the Ethiopian (Acts 8:6-40) who wanted to be baptized WHILE he was still hearing about the gospel from Phillip?

The emphasis the Bible places on baptism should be the guiding factor on how important it is. In the first century church of the New Testament, you would be hard-pressed to find any Christian who was not baptized. Baptism was an immediate, natural progression or step for someone professing that Jesus was their Lord and Savior. This marked their profession of faith and marked them among the body of believers (Matthew 28:19-20; Acts 2:38).

As important as being baptized is to the new believer, it is equally as important on how you should be baptized. In Romans 6:3-7, Paul paints a great picture of what baptism by immersion represents.

> *3 "Or do you not know that all of us who have been baptized into Christ Jesus have been baptized into His death? 4 Therefore we have been buried with Him through baptism into death, so that as Christ was raised from the dead through the glory of the Father, so we too might walk in newness of life. 5 For if we have become united with Him in the likeness of His death, certainly we shall also be in the likeness of His resurrection, 6 knowing this, that our old self was crucified with Him, in order that our body of sin might be done away with, so that we would no longer be slaves to sin; 7 for he who has died is freed from sin."*

BAPTISM BY IMMERSION IN WATER IS YOUR PUBLIC ACKNOWLEDGMENT OF DEATH TO YOUR SIN AND YOUR RESURRECTION INTO NEW LIFE IN CHRIST.

This scripture shows us the spiritual reality of our union with Christ and how we are one with Him during His death AND resurrection. Baptism by immersion in water is your public acknowledgment of death to your sin and your resurrection into new life in Christ. Unfortunately, because there are so many "false" theologies about baptism being taught today, there are a LOT of professing believers who haven't been baptized. If you are one of those unfortunate believers who has not participated in a baptism by immersion, it's critical that you carefully and biblically evaluate your life and figure out why you are unwilling to publicly identify with Christ. Choosing NOT to do so is to be in open disobedience to the Word of God, regardless of the excuses you may be telling yourself.

You need to repent and be baptized. What are you waiting for?

Chapter Five

Who are you calling, "Buttercup?"

"Pursue love, and desire spiritual gifts, but especially that you may prophesy." ~ 1 Corinthians 14:1

The first time I ever received a word from God was spoken through another person in 2008 while I was visiting my friends Ben and Michelle in Oxford, England. I had arrived the previous day and on that day they were hosting their small group from church. We were all sitting around chatting and sharing the details of our week, when John, one of the pastors in their church, called this lady in the group out and said he had a word from the Lord for her. A word from the Lord? Was he serious? I can't remember what he said to her because I thought it was a little odd, but it wasn't directed at me; so I didn't really pay much attention.

That is, until he turned to me and said, "*Rachel, I have a word for YOU, as well.*" I remember thinking, "*Who? Me? What is he talking about? How does he even know my name?*"

He began to speak. "*Rachel, you see yourself as a small buttercup, all alone in the middle of a large field.*"

Ok, wait a minute here. If this was really God, He would NEVER use buttercup to describe me, because I certainly would not have chosen that name to describe myself. Wasn't He supposed to know me better than I know myself? Then, I started to worry about what Michelle may have been thinking. I could just picture what was going on in her mind, "*Poor Rachel. She's alone and won't even admit to herself that she's alone; I knew that her denial was not how she truly felt. We have to find someone for her."* (I know that wasn't true, but that's what I was thinking at the time). At the same time, I was thinking there was no way this guy was receiving a word from the Lord for me.

He continued, *"But God sees you, Rachel, as a man-sized buttercup (there's that word again) with thousands and thousands of little buttercups all around you."* Huh? What was he trying to tell me?

We finished the evening with a lesson, some worship music, and dessert, but I couldn't stop thinking about what John had said to me. It consumed me. It really did!

After everyone had left, Michelle turned to me and asked, *"Hey, you wanna watch a movie?"* Watch a movie? Is she kidding? I was totally freaked out and I didn't know how to talk about it. I politely declined, saying, *"No. I'm really tired Mich. I think I will just head off to bed. See you in the morning?"*

She replied, *"Of course. See you in the morning. Sleep well!"*

I went to my room and didn't fall asleep for 3-4 hours. It was a long night. I could not stop thinking about what Pastor John had said to me and I was slightly embarrassed by it. Embarrassed by what you may be asking? First of all, being referred to as a buttercup! That is one of the last things on the planet I would use to describe myself, so I began to wonder if that was truly how people saw me. Of course, there WAS the thought that maybe it WAS from the Lord. If so, what in the world, did it mean? I certainly did not want to be a missionary - been down that road and I hoped to never experience THAT again! Did I really feel alone? Was I in denial? I didn't think so. I had finally gotten to a point in my life where I was content. These thoughts and many others kept rolling around in my mind. It's a wonder I ever fell asleep, but I calmed myself by thinking I would talk about it with Michelle in the morning.

The next day came and went. I NEVER brought it up and neither did she. I was still in a mild state of anxiety, but I had found a way to cope with it. That night, I slept a little better, but mostly because I was so tired from not sleeping the night before and still feeling jet-lagged.

On Friday, Michelle and I hopped a double decker bus to go and tour London for the day. This was my first double decker bus ride ever, so it already had some significance for me.

Five minutes into the ride, I turned and looked at Michelle and said, "*Could we please talk about the elephant in the room?*" "*Sure. Which elephant would you like to talk about?*" she said with a smile (as IF there were ANY other elephant to talk about). "*You know,... the "word" John gave to me the other night,*" I said, feeling all of the anxiety come to the top as I was finally going to talk about what I had been struggling with for the past 36 hours. "*Oh?* (Pause for effect) *What do you want to know?*"

"*Do you know what 'the word' meant or what he was talking about?*" I asked her.

"*Yes*", she replied

"*Awesome!*" I said. "*Thank God! I have been thinking about it ever since John said it. What did he mean?*" She waited a moment, which I might add felt like forever, and then she said, "*I'm not going to tell you, Rach.*"

Incredulously, I replied, "*What? You know what it means and you're not going to tell me? ARE YOU SERIOUS?*" Then I turned away from her, crossed my arms and pouted. After a good five minutes, I uncrossed my arms and turned to her expectantly. She just gave me a look and said, "*Are you done?*"

"*Yes. I'm sorry.*" I sheepishly replied. In my heart, I knew I did not want something like this to ruin the rest of my trip and I certainly didn't want it to affect our friendship.

She said, "*Listen Rach, if you really want me to explain it to you, I will. But just know that I really feel like God is trying to talk to you and HE wants to explain it all to you.*"

Great! There's no way I'm going to ask her to explain it to me now, even though, she DID say she would. What troubled me the most about it was I didn't feel like God EVER communicated with me, so how would I EVER get this figured out? Either way, I made a decision right then and there that I wasn't going to spend any more time stressing about it while I was visiting with Michelle in England. There would be plenty of time on the plane ride home to spend time thinking about it, waiting/hoping for God to answer.

The following Sunday, I attended Ben & Michelle's church. I think it was called the King's Church. After meeting a lot of their friends, we found our place in the front row, off to the right and began to worship. When the singing was finished, we sat down and someone in the center of the church stood up and began speaking in another language. I had been to many churches, where people attempted to "demonstrate" speaking in tongues, but it always sounded like a bunch nonsense to me, but not this time. It actually sounded like a language, even though I couldn't understand it. The exciting thing for me was when a second person stood up on the other side of the church and actually translated what was said! Just like it is described in the scriptures! I was so excited; I could hardly contain myself. Michelle just kept laughing at me because I kept asking her, "*Did that just happen? Did someone just speak in "tongues" AND someone actually translated it?*"

"*Yes, Rach, that's what just happened,*" she laughed.

I could hardly believe it! I knew, without a shadow of a doubt, that I had just experienced the first century church in Oxford, England in 2008, and I was NEVER going to forget that moment! Little did I know how the Holy Spirit would use that trip to change my life!

The rest of the trip to England was spiritually uneventful. I had a great time visiting a country I had never been to before and spending quality time with people who I loved and adored. It was fascinating to look at a culture that was similar to my own, but very different as well.

So, I made it back to the states and was now thoroughly convinced that God wanted me to be a missionary. What kind of missionary, I didn't know. Where would I go? I didn't know that either, but I was convinced, that was what God wanted and I really wasn't all that excited about it. I was also still struggling with the word "buttercup" used to describe me.

A few weeks later, while I was reading my Bible, the Spirit suggested I go and look up the word buttercup online. So, I stopped what I was doing and headed to the computer to do just that. What I found amazed me! Buttercups are different from the other flowers in the way that they reproduce. Most flowers have one stamen to reproduce from, while the buttercups have up to 20 stamens. When I finished reading, the Holy Spirit quietly explained to me that I was going to be able to reproduce what He was planting in me over and over again, very quickly and in large quantities. He said it was my responsibility to keep those flowers in bloom by staying fertilized by His Presence.

This trip to England appeared on the surface as just another opportunity to visit another part of the world and to spend some quality time with some very special people. When in reality, it was divinely designed to bring me into an amazing relationship with the Holy Spirit! This trip got me all fired up about learning about and from the Holy Spirit! I couldn't believe that something so exciting wasn't being taught from every pulpit around the world.

What if I responded differently? What if I didn't seek out the Holy Spirit's confirmation? Being a new Christian, and very immature in my understanding of the Holy Spirit, I wasted a lot of energy trying to figure out what was being said to me. Was it from God or not? What did it mean? You get the idea.

There's a Bible story in 2nd Kings, chapter five about a man named Naaman who was healed after "receiving a word" from the prophet Elisha. Naaman was an honorable man and well respected by the King of Syria because he was an outstanding commander of the Syrian army. Unfortunately, he had one major flaw - he had leprosy, which sometimes hindered his ability to lead.

One day, he found out through his wife's servant girl (who happened to be an Israelite) that he could receive healing from the prophet Elisha. After receiving permission from the King, he traveled to see the prophet Elisha in hopes that he would heal him. When he arrived at the prophet's door, he didn't even get to see the prophet. Instead, he was instructed by Elisha's messenger to go to the Jordan River and wash seven times. Naaman became angry and almost missed out on his healing because he felt that this silly little ritual would never bring his desired healing.

However, after much convincing from his OWN servant, he begrudgingly followed the directions of the prophet Elisha and amazingly, after the seventh dip, he was miraculously healed!

Interestingly enough, I kind of felt like Naaman when I received that word of the Lord from John, but in a different way. Someone (Pastor John) was attempting to speak into my life as if the message came from God. He used words and terminology that made it very easy for me to be upset or even ignore the word he said was meant for me. I mean, the word "buttercup" literally almost sent me over the edge.

Have you ever received a word from someone or had someone try to speak into your life and wondered, *"What do I do with that? THAT can't be from the Lord!"* Even more interesting, have you ever felt impressed to share something with someone else about their life or their journey? Do you wonder if you are supposed to share it or not? Was it REALLY from the Holy Spirit or just your desire to encourage someone?

I think Naaman was extremely happy that he followed the words of the prophet instead of wallowing in offense because this man did not bring healing in the manner that he expected or desired. It was his obedience and his reluctant faith that opened the door for God to bring healing. It had nothing to do with the water nor the amount of washing.

Here's the deal, whenever we receive a word from somebody, it is our responsibility to listen. It doesn't matter if they are off their rocker, crazy as a loon, or just plain wrong. We need to hear the word. God will use all kinds of people and all kinds of ways to communicate with us. That's ok. He's God and He can use anyone He wishes.

GOD WILL USE ALL KINDS OF PEOPLE AND ALL KINDS OF WAYS TO COMMUNICATE WITH US.

My word came from a Pastor - someone who has credibility because he carries the title of pastor. However, he was a pastor who didn't know me nor did I know him. My mistake was getting all worked up about it, getting worried that this was THE word of God for my entire life and that it needed to be figured out right now. The proper response would have been to just listen. I didn't need to change anything in my life or focus on all the potential meanings of certain words (like "buttercup" or "feeling all alone"). I just needed to listen. After hearing the word, I needed to pray a simple prayer to Holy Spirit. Something like,

"Holy Spirit, is this something you are trying to bring to my attention? If it is, will You speak it to me and confirm it? If not, will You just take it away?"

Afterwards, I just needed to move on and trust that the same Holy Spirit who MAY have placed that word within the other person, lives inside of me, too! Therefore, if it WAS from Him (which, by the way, I believe it was), He will definitely make it known to me personally. How cool is that?

Now, if you are on the other side of things and are really feeling impressed to share an impression or a word with another person, just follow the scriptures and run it through James 3:17:

> But the wisdom that is from above is first pure, then peaceable, gentle, willing to yield, full of mercy and good fruits, without partiality and without hypocrisy."

If it's truly from Holy Spirit, it has to fit within the parameters of this scripture. Now, if it doesn't fall within the parameters of James 3:17, don't speak it. Sometimes, Holy Spirit wants to reveal something to us so we can pray for that individual. It's important to understand that not everything revealed is meant to be shared.

IT'S IMPORTANT TO UNDERSTAND THAT NOT EVERYTHING REVEALED IS MEANT TO BE SHARED.

For some amazing reason, God LOVES people and LOVES to work through them. So, don't be surprised when He gives you a word for someone else or if someone else is given a word for you. If you're the giver, remember to run it past James 3:17 and if you are the receiver, just ask Holy Spirit to confirm or deny it and then act accordingly.

Holy Spirit is speaking! Are you listening?

Chapter Six

Finding Living Faith

"By this all will know that you are My disciples, if you have love for one another." ~ John 13:35

Upon returning from London, England, I had developed a huge appetite for the Holy Spirit. While with Ben & Michelle at the King's Church in Oxford, England, I saw people speaking in tongues and others interpreting, people were speaking words into other's lives straight from the heart of God, and the worship was amazingly authentic. They had a Bible college that taught healings, miracles, and deliverance from demons among other things. The people there were walking in the nine gifts of the Holy Spirit talked about in 1 Corinthians 12 and I wanted to experience that, too! I wanted to know Holy Spirit, love Him, and work with Him, but I hadn't found anyone that was teaching about Him or more importantly, using His power. The three years between choosing Jesus as my Lord and Savior and my trip to England in 2008, had taken me all over northern Virginia looking for a church and never finding one that felt like home.

Just before going to England, I had sort of chosen a local church to call home, but I struggled to fit in there and they didn't offer any classes on the Holy Spirit, which left me frustrated and disappointed. My mom suggested that I do a Google search for an Apostolic Church in northern Virginia. When I did, Living Faith Church was the very first link (http://www.livingbyfaith.com) to pop up, so I clicked on it. As I kept looking around their website, I got more and more excited! I can't really give you a good reason why, except maybe, it was because they had a Ministry Training Center that offered a 2-year certificate program and a 4-year diploma program. It didn't matter; everything I read just seemed to get me excited and kept me excited. There was so much that I wanted to know, so many questions I needed answered.

It took another three weeks before I was able to make it to a service. Each Sunday was filled with one excuse or another. One week I was working. The next week I was traveling and I was getting a little frustrated! Here was a church that I was finally excited to go check out and I couldn't even get there!

Thankfully, this did not concern the Holy Spirit at all. He knew which day He wanted me to be there. It was a Tuesday at the beginning of August 2008. I finished work a little earlier than usual, so I made the random decision to go to their weekly evening service. I actually got there a little early and strangely enough, I was a little nervous. Seems silly to me at first, because I had been to a LOT of churches over the past 3 years, but now as I think about it, I realize I was just really afraid of being disappointed. Talk about wasted energy!

As I was getting out of my Jeep, a friend of a friend walked up to me and invited me to sit with her during the service. I didn't even know that she attended church there, but I was glad to see a familiar face to ease some of my anxiety. I enjoyed the time of worship. They have an amazing worship team that ushered in a sweet presence that I have since come to recognize as the Holy Spirit. This was a great precursor to the evening's message presented by Pastor Barry Lubbe, the "father" of this house. His topic for the evening was on the Baptism of the Holy Spirit with the evidence of speaking in tongues. Can you believe it? This is exactly what I had been searching and hungering for since I returned from England. Right here, under my nose, in my hometown!

I sat there in awe and wonder at how the Holy Spirit had worked out the entire encounter. How incredible was that! I was there on the very night when the service would be ALL about the Holy

Spirit! Thank You Holy Spirit for orchestrating my life to continually find You and be found by You.

My friend Elizabeth, who I wrote about in an earlier chapter, told me that when I found where God wanted me to be planted, I would know. I didn't believe her. Fortunately, she was right. That evening, I KNEW that I KNEW that I KNEW that THIS was supposed to be my church, and I have never looked back! Three days later, I met with Pastor Cathy, the dean of the Ministry Training Center, to sign up for classes. My life has never been the same since I took that step of faith and walked through those doors.

You see, it's very important to find a place that we can fellowship with other like-minded people. When we spend time with other Christians, we become encouraged in our faith and realize that we're not alone in our struggles or our joys. Good Christian friends and/or mentors will caution us

IT'S VERY IMPORTANT TO FIND A PLACE THAT WE CAN FELLOWSHIP WITH OTHER LIKE-MINDED PEOPLE.

when they see things taking us off the chosen path. Without these believers, we might easily miss the warning on how a particular teaching or behavior could be damaging to our faith.

Spending time with other believers helps us to refocus. Our friends WILL affect us, whether we like it or not. Choosing to spend time with Christians and limiting time with friends that distract us from God is a sign that God is working in us and that we are willing to surrender.

So, How Do I Find a Good Church?

If you base your decision on just two characteristics, you will find the search a lot less stressful and discouraging. They are TRUTH and LOVE -- these are necessary if a church is going to help you grow in your relationship with God.

The truth you are looking for is based on the Word of God (aka the Bible). Do they recognize it as the ultimate authority in their mission? Is the Bible used and/or quoted in their services and their classes? Does worship reflect who God is? Are people growing and maturing in their faith? Are the members exhibiting the fruit of the Spirit in their lives?

Let's not forget that truth must be balanced with love (1 Corinthians 13:13). Does the church demonstrate love within the church? How about the community or even the world? Love in action is a great way to demonstrate that God's truth is a part of their lives. Do people serve and care for each other? Is the church concerned with the spiritual needs of the world around them? Living Faith confesses and believes:

"Northern Virginia WILL BE SAVED."

Loving others shows that we belong to God (John 13:34-35).

As you are making the decision of where to go to church, remember to ask God to help you select the right one. He will gladly provide wisdom and discernment as you choose which church to call "home".

Chapter Seven

Baptism by the Holy Spirit

"But ye shall receive power, after the Holy Ghost is come upon you." ~ Acts 1:8

The day that I found Living Faith Church was a day with a lot of excitement and anticipation. I had finally found the place where Jesus wanted me to be planted. AND it had a ministry training center, too! I was so excited I could barely contain myself! They had a two or four year program where I could immerse myself in everything Holy Spirit (Father God & Jesus, too).

I showed up to my interview a little early. I was so excited, but really nervous. Interviewing for acceptance to get into a school was nothing new to me, but for some reason, I wanted to be a part of this school more than any other school I had ever attended. After reading this book, you will understand why.

The interview went well. About halfway into the interview, Pastor Cathy asked me if I had ever received the baptism of the Holy Spirit. Now, I had heard of it before, but I didn't really understand what that meant and I told her so. She spent some time explaining it more in detail and then asked me again, "*Would you like to receive the baptism of the Holy Spirit?*" What else could I say, but "*I guess so.*" She came around her desk, sat down beside me, and asked if she could lay her hands on me. I responded, "*Sure.*" With that permission, she laid one hand on the top of my head and the other on the back of my right shoulder and began to speak in a language I had never heard before. Kind of weirded me out, if I'm being completely honest.

It sounded like a language, just not one that I knew or understood.

After a few minutes, she stopped and invited me to speak in MY new language. I didn't get it. I had no idea what that meant or how to make that happen, and I told her that, too. She gently encouraged me to open my mouth and speak whatever came. So, I opened my mouth and I sat there, looking around the room. It didn't occur to me that I had to make the effort. The Holy Spirit is such the gentleman; He will never overtake you, without your permission. We waited a few minutes and I could feel the anxiety rising up on the inside of me. "*Maybe God didn't want me to have it,*" I thought, "*Or I must be doing something wrong.*" Of course, those were lies straight from the pit of hell and Pastor Cathy told me so.

She prayed some more and then encouraged me to try again. I was still unsuccessful. In fact, by the time I left, I still had not received the manifestation of speaking in tongues. However, I knew something remarkable had happened. When Pastor Cathy laid her hand on my shoulder, it felt like fire was coming through her hand straight into my shoulder. It was so intense; I thought for sure there would be a bright red burn mark on my shoulder where her hand had been. There was never a burn mark. In fact, there wasn't any pain associated with it at all.

Now rest assured, I did receive the manifestation of the baptism of the Holy Spirit with the evidence of speaking in tongues. It actually started from six syllables and progressed to a full language a few weeks later, while I was immersed in worship at the training center. My mind had been so wrapped up in religious tradition. This was a new teaching, a new concept for me and it took a little bit of time to get it through this thick skull. Talk about an encounter with Holy Spirit - being touched with fire from the hand of God!

So, What is this Baptism of the Holy Spirit?

Every Christian is born of the Spirit. When we are "born again", our original spirit dies with sin and a new spirit is regenerated in us by the Holy Spirit (1 Corinthians 5:17). As you will hopefully see, this is NOT the same as receiving the Baptism of the Holy Spirit. Father God wants to give His children a dimension of power that can only be received through the baptism of the Holy Spirit (Acts 2:38-39).

There are many Christians who achieve much without this baptism, I can't even begin to imagine how much harder it is for a pastor or an evangelist to function in their calling without this additional power. Imagine how much lighter their work would be if they were functioning in their calling with the POWER of the Holy Spirit!

Now, some Christians believe that the baptism of the Holy Spirit is not for us today. While others believe that every "born again" Christian was baptized at conversion. Both of these belief systems rob Christians of part of their inheritance. We, as Christians (or believers) are very good at receiving the first part of our inheritance through the blood of Jesus Christ. However, we miss out on the second part that comes through the resurrection of Jesus Christ - the Holy Spirit! I don't know about you, but I want ALL that Jesus has for me!

Take a look at how the Bible shows us that the regeneration of our spirits (aka "born again") is not the same as receiving the Baptism of the Holy Spirit.

1. Jesus' disciples received the spirit of regeneration before Jesus ascended when He breathed on them and told them to "Receive the Holy Spirit". (John 20:22) This is when they were born again (received their new spirits or became a new creation). However, notice that this was BEFORE Pentecost. Jesus told them to wait for the promise of the Father (Acts 1:4), the baptism of the Holy

Spirit (Acts 1:5). This occurred at Pentecost AFTER they were born again AND after Jesus had ascended to the Father.

Acts 1:4,5 – **4** *"And being assembled together with them, He commanded them not to depart from Jerusalem, but to* wait for the Promise of the Father, *"which" He said, "you have heard from Me* **5** *for John truly baptized with water, but* you shall be baptized with the Holy Spirit *not many days from now."* (emphasis added)

2. The Samaritans believed the gospel and were baptized (Acts 8:12). THEN they received the baptism of the Holy Spirit when Peter and John realized that they had yet to receive it (Acts 8:14-17). Moreover, if you read just a little further in that same chapter, this power was so impressive that Simon the magician wanted to buy it! It was NOT some quiet blessing!

Acts 8:14-17 – **14** *"Now when the apostles who were at Jerusalem heard that Samaria had received the word of God, they sent Peter and John to them,* **15** *who, when they had come down, prayed for them that they might receive the Holy Spirit.* **16** *For as yet He had fallen upon none of them. They had only been baptized in the name of the Lord Jesus.* **17** *Then they laid hands on them, and they received the Holy Spirit."*

3. Paul was born again when he confessed Jesus as Lord (Acts 9:3-8; Romans 10:9). Three days later, Paul received both his vision AND the baptism of the Holy Spirit when Ananias laid hands on him.

Acts 9:17 – *"And Ananias went his way and entered the house and laying his hands on him he said, "Brother Saul, the Lord Jesus, who appeared to you on the road as you came, has sent me that you may receive your sight and be filled with the Holy Spirit."*

[51]

4. Now, Cornelius and his household (Acts 10:44-47) received the baptism of the Holy Spirit at the same time that they were born again. How do we know?

Acts 10:44-47 – **44** *"While Peter was still speaking these words, the Holy Spirit fell upon all those who heard the word.* **45** *And those of the circumcision who believed were astonished, as many as came with Peter, because the gift of the Holy Spirit had been poured out on the Gentiles also.* **46** *For they heard them speak with tongues and magnify God. Then Peter answered,* **47** *"Can anyone forbid water, that these should not be baptized who have received the Holy Spirit just as we have?"*

Peter realized that they had received the SAME baptism of the Holy Spirit as the disciples did at Pentecost (Acts 11:15-16)!

In the Bible, speaking in an unknown tongue is the sign that a person had indeed received the baptism of the Holy Spirit (Acts 2:4; Acts 10:46; Acts 19:6; Mark 16:17). Even Paul said that he spoke more in tongues than ANY other Christian did (1 Corinthians 14:18). The Bible says,

"*Desire earnestly to prophesy, and do not forbid to speak with tongues.*" (1 Corinthians 14:39)

The Ephesians did this as exhibited in Acts 19:6.

"*And when Paul laid hands on them, the Holy Spirit came upon them, and they spoke with tongues and prophesied.*"

You see, the Holy Spirit empowers our Christian walk. He teaches us and leads us into all truth (John 16:13).

How many times in your life have you gone before the Father to discuss a situation with Him and really didn't know what to say or where to start? I can tell you that there have been MANY times

I have found myself in that very predicament, at least before I received the baptism of the Holy Spirit.

What I have found is that when I yield my tongue to Him, He sorts it out and brings out the perfect prayer for the situation (Romans 8:26-27). He sees the big picture, I don't. When I defer to Him, I pray the perfect prayer and the perfect will of God. Therefore, I find my prayers are more productive. Sometimes, the Holy Spirit has brought unconfessed sins to my mind or has shown me spirits that are torturing or controlling me or someone else.

WHAT I HAVE FOUND IS THAT WHEN I YIELD MY TONGUE TO HIM, HE SORTS IT OUT AND BRINGS OUT THE PERFECT PRAYER FOR THE SITUATION.

If you would like to receive the baptism of the Holy Spirit, then say this prayer out loud.

Jesus, I want ALL of you and ALL that you have promised me. Thank You for the gift of salvation. Baptize me with Your Holy Spirit like you did to those in the early church. I am a believer and You said that believers would speak in unknown tongues. So, I give my life to You and I open my heart to You, right now, I receive this promised Gift of the baptism of the Holy Spirit. Thank You, Jesus - AMEN!

Now spend some time focusing on Jesus. Your step of faith is to open your mouth and start to make syllables you don't understand. Trust that the Holy Spirit will guide those syllables into His perfect prayer and watch how your life will begin to change.

Chapter Eight

Prayers that Heal the Heart

"Do not rejoice over me, my enemy; When I fall, I will arise; When I sit in darkness, the Lord will be a light to me." ~ Micah 7:8

I had the privilege of meeting with Sally at Living Faith Church and to work through a particular ministry called "Prayers That Heal the Heart." We talked about a lot of different things like lies I had believed, vows I made because of those lies, ungodly soul ties, generational curses, sin, etc. It was such an amazing and freeing experience.

During one of our earlier sessions, I had a vision of when I was a baby still in the womb, filled with fear. I could see these black creatures, a lot of them, flying at me from a distance. The closer they got, the uglier and scarier they became. I remember feeling very afraid and knowing there was nothing I could do about it. Somehow, I knew they had a right to be there, though. They were coming to get me and I knew they were going to be successful. The closer they got, the more afraid I became. I could feel that fear seeping into the deepest parts of me and I did not like it one bit.

I cried out for help. Within seconds, I saw this bright light emanating from directly above me. It kept getting brighter and brighter until it enveloped me entirely. The warmth and love I felt was incredible! It kept growing, getting bigger and bigger and brighter and brighter. Until finally, the cross appeared from within the light. It popped up from the "ground" and provided a barrier between the ugly black creatures and me. All of a sudden there was absolute pandemonium on the other side of the cross as those black creatures began scrambling about, trying to figure out how to get past the cross to me. Then the best thing happened! The cross crushed those ugly black creatures, like a game of whack-a-mole. It was one of the most incredible things I have ever experienced. The peace I felt knowing that I was being protected from things that were beyond my control is difficult to explain. Jesus said that His peace would be a peace that defies all understanding (Philippians 4:7) and it's an amazing gift to experience.

The black creatures were gone. The cross was firmly in position and I continued to be swallowed in the light and love of God. Then the vision ended. I could have stayed and rested in that vision a lot longer. It was incredible!

That evening when I got home, I decided to lay before Holy Spirit and ask Him about the truth that was presented to me during my session with Sally. Did He really love me that much? Has God always loved me? Was I really special to Him?

He took me to scriptures that talked about love and invited me to read Psalm 91. Have you ever spent time in that passage? It talks about the safety that comes to us when we abide in the presence of God!

> *1 He who dwells in the secret place of the Most High Shall abide under the shadow of the Almighty. 2 I will say of the LORD, "He is my refuge and my fortress; My God, in Him I will trust."* ~ Psalm 91:1-2

To be tucked under the shadow of God → That's me! I am safe in His arms, under His shadow, His umbrella of protection. The Holy Spirit then whispered to me, "*Recognize and trust My love for what it is.*" So, I asked Him what love was and He told me to turn to 1 John, chapter 4 and to read verses 7 through 19. When I did, this is what I read.

Knowing God Through Love

> *7 Beloved, let us love one another, for love is of God; and everyone who loves is born of God and knows God. 8 He who does not love does not know God, for God is love. 9 In this the love of God was manifested toward us, that God has sent His only begotten Son into the world, that we might live through Him. 10 In this is love, not that we loved God, but that He loved us and sent His Son to be the propitiation for our sins. 11 Beloved, if God so loved us, we also ought to love one another.*

Seeing God Through Love

> *12 No one has seen God at any time. If we love one another, God abides in us, and His love has been perfected in us. 13 By this we know that we abide In Him, and He in us, because He has given us of His Spirit. 14 And we have seen and testify that the Father has sent the Son as Savior of the world. 15 Whoever confesses that Jesus is the Son of God, God abides in him, and he in God. 16 And we have known and believed the love that God has for us. God is love, and he who abides in love abides in God, and God in him.*

The Consummation of Love

> *17 Love has been perfected among us in this: that we may have boldness in the day of judgment; because as He is, so are we in this world. 18 There is no fear in love; but perfect love casts out fear, because fear involves torment. But he who fears has not been made perfect in love. 19 We love Him because He first loved us.*

Now, I've read that passage many times before, but it never had as much of an impact on me as it did that time. God is love. So, what He said to me just before referring me to this passage could have just as easily said, "*Recognize and trust God for Who He is!"* because God is love. Wow! I sat there for a few minutes and let that roll around in my mind. Holy Spirit was presenting me with personal revelation, a personal understanding of what this scripture holds for His children.

This is what I found when I continued reading in Psalm 91.

> *3 Surely He shall deliver you from the snare of the fowler And from the perilous pestilence. 4 He shall cover you with His feathers, And under His wings you shall take refuge; His truth shall be your shield and buckler. 5 You shall not be afraid of the terror by night, Nor of the arrow that flies by day, 6 Nor of the pestilence that walks in darkness, Nor of the destruction that lays waste at noonday.* ~ Psalm 91:3-6

I didn't really know what the snare of a fowler was or what perilous pestilence meant, but what I did know is they didn't sound very good. For all intents and purposes, their meanings didn't really matter much to me at the time, because Holy Spirit was showing me how much He loved me by promising to deliver me (and you, too) from all of those terrible things!

During the session with Sally earlier that day, we had broken a lot of ungodly soul ties and generational curses. Each time we did, I SAW Jesus placing the cross at the entrance to my life, as a guard, and a protector against ALL of these attacks. The enemy cannot return because the cross permanently blocks the way. He and his demons have already been defeated! Each time those black creatures tried to get past the cross, they were repelled by its power and majesty. The cross had never become as real to me as it did at that moment. Thank You, Holy Spirit!

I want to recommend that you finish reading the rest of Psalm 91 and ask Holy Spirit to reveal to YOUR heart what He is trying to say to YOU. Substituting YOUR name in the passage will allow it to become more personal to you and open greater revelation. For example,

14 "Because she (Rachel) has set his (her) love upon Me (Jesus), therefore I (Jesus) will deliver her (Rachel); I (Jesus) will set her (Rachel) on high, because she (Rachel) has known My name. 15 She (Rachel) shall call upon Me (Jesus), and I (Jesus) will answer her (Rachel), I (Jesus) will be with her (Rachel) in trouble; I (Jesus) will deliver her (Rachel) and honor her (Rachel). 16 With long life I (Jesus) will satisfy her (Rachel), And show her (Rachel) My (Jesus) salvation."

Holy Spirit also led me to read Psalm 139. This is what He revealed to my heart.

God knows me. God knew me before He made me. God knew me when I was only a substance, before He formed me in my mother's womb. He knew and knows my thoughts and most importantly, He knows my heart.

God has always loved me! I have always been special to Him. I am a priority to Him That is why He has been pursuing me all of these years.

God is very personal and He wants to spend time with you. He thinks about you ALL the time. He loves you! He has never rejected you, nor will He ever. Come to Him! Practice being in His presence. Eyes toward God opens the flow of the Holy Spirit. The enemy (satan) causes you to be bent over with all of his lies. When you are bent over, you no longer have your eyes on Jesus. Stand up, my friend, look up and focus on Jesus. This opens the path to allow Holy Spirit to flow through you.

To wrap up this chapter, I want to share two of the lies that I believed about myself and how Holy Spirit brought truth into the situation to set me free. The first lie was that I was unlovable. In my quiet time, Holy Spirit revealed to me that I am, indeed, loved AND loveable. This (that I was unlovable) was a lie from satan used to hinder me from becoming who Father God created me to be.

So, I asked Him, "*Holy Spirit, I know this is a lie (that I was unlovable) from satan. Please reveal to me Your truth about this and about me.*"

This was His response.

"*Rachel, my child. YOU are an awesome creation! It was from the pure love and joy in MY heart that became the center of your being. With that truth, you should see that you could NEVER be unlovable. My daughter, how I treasure you! You were created for great things in My Kingdom! My hands lovingly created you in your mother's womb and my angels have closely protected you from birth. Yes, mistakes have been made, but you live in a fallen world and because of that, I STILL love you! I STILL love you... did you get that? STILL infers that I have had to love you prior to now, AND I WILL CONTINUE to do so. I have loved you from the moment I thought about you, the moment I envisioned you.*

Oh, Rachel, I have been excited for your time on earth. You have the heart like my servant David, so tender, so full of love...... it's time for the full expression of My love to flow forth into your heart and into the hearts of all those around you. We are going to change the world together! Will you take My hand and follow me?"

I replied, "*Yes, Lord! I will follow You!*"

He continued, "*Rachel, I love you, I LOVE you! I LOVE YOU! Allow that seed to plant deep within your heart. I will nurture it and grow it and you won't have the ability to keep it inside.*"

I answered, "*Father, I receive this seed of Your love into my heart. I ask that you seal it there and nurture it! And allow me the opportunity, no, the privilege, of sharing this love, Your love, with everyone I meet!*"

The other lie that we uncovered during that session was my belief that the world is a terrible place. So, I asked Holy Spirit, "*Please reveal your truth about this to me.*"

He responded with this, "*Rachel, this world is My creation for you. It only becomes a bad place when you come into agreement with satan and/or one of his minions. I AM BIGGER than all of them together! I have overcome the world! YOU belong to me and they are not permitted to touch what is Mine! I am your protector and your fortress. You are the love of my life. Trust in me. I will keep you safe. I will bring you peace. I will be your strong tower. In Me, there is nothing you cannot do or accomplish →therefore, YOUR world WILL be a safe environment and I will protect you and all those in your circle.*"

Ok, you may be wondering why I have chosen to share these with you. It's pretty personal. Well, I shared it because I want you to understand my heart. Relationship with Holy Spirit does not have to be hard. He created us for relationship and longs to have conversations with us. For me, at times, it is easier to write what I hear Him saying so I can compare what the Bible has to say about what I'm hearing. If it doesn't match up with the Word of God, then I can be certain that it did not come from God. Would you like to test that out for yourself? Go ahead and try it! Take MY words written above and compare them with what the Word of God says. Then, once you do that, I would encourage you to try it for yourself. Get before Holy Spirit and ask Him about something that has been bothering you. Write down what you hear and then search the Bible and see if it flows with what the Word says!

IF IT DOESN'T MATCH UP WITH THE WORD OF GOD, THEN I CAN BE CERTAIN THAT IT DID NOT COME FROM GOD.

Chapter Nine

Healing at Work

"Now God worked unusual miracles by the hands of Paul, so that even handkerchiefs or aprons were brought from his body to the sick, and the diseases left them and the evil spirits went out of them."
~ Acts 19:11-12

Working as an emergency nurse in Northern Virginia has afforded me many amazing opportunities to meet a lot of different people. For five years, I rotated through every emergency department throughout the northern Virginia area. It was an amazing and exciting time! In addition, I had just completed my first two classes (one was on healing and the other was on the righteousness of Christ) in the Ministry Training Center. I was so excited about God, about life; I was excited about everything, really.

One day I was working in one of the local emergency departments, when a 24-year-old guy came into the ER with chest tightness, a little shortness of breath, and a LOT of anxiety. Upon further examination, he was found to be in an irregular heartbeat known as Atrial Fibrillation.

The human heart is composed of four chambers that hold blood. The top two chambers are known as the atria. This is where the blood is held, briefly, until it is pushed into the ventricles, which are the two bottom chambers of the heart. They pump the blood to the rest of the body. In a normal functioning heart, the atria makes the "LUB" sound of your heartbeat, while the ventricles make the "DUB" sound of your heartbeat, for a combined sound of "LUB DUB".

However, in Atrial Fibrillation, the atria is quivering instead of pumping. It is no longer effectively moving the blood to the ventricles. Blood begins to collect in pools within the atria and whenever blood sits still, it forms clots! These clots travel throughout the body and can cause heart attacks, strokes, and even blood clots in the lungs. So, as you can see, Atrial Fibrillation can develop into a serious problem very quickly. We needed to resolve it fast.

This patient had actually been assigned to another nurse when he presented to the ER, but since the doctors were struggling to convert his rhythm back, the charge nurse asked me to assist the nurse with the patient.

When I walked into the room, there were two doctors standing in front of the defibrillator (an instrument that sends electricity to the heart to shock it back into a normal rhythm), discussing what to do next. He had already been shocked six times without success. Since he was only 24 years old, there was no reason for him to be in that rhythm. Now that he was, he should have converted rather quickly. I could hear the doctors talking about admitting him for further testing. Even though the patient was properly sedated, the RN at his bedside was a little shaken because he had been shocked so many times.

After speaking with her for a moment, I walked over to the patient, laid my hand on his chest where his heart was located, and commanded it in the name of Jesus to return to a normal rhythm and to NEVER slip into atrial fibrillation again! I spoke with barely a whisper and within 30 seconds, the patient converted back to a normal rhythm without any further shocks or assistance from the doctors. A large smile spread across my face.

As I turned around, the nurse in the room whispered under her breath with amazement, "*What did you just do? I heard you say something and then his heartbeat converted! WHAT was THAT?*"

I chuckled a little, and told her to come find me later and I would explain everything to her. Thankfully, she was a Christian, so it was much easier to explain. Within an hour, the patient was discharged home. Isn't God amazing? He used the hands of a baby Christian to bring healing to a young man who needed it right then and there.

Ok, let me be the first to tell you, this was the very first time that the Holy Spirit had used me to bring healing to someone else. I was only in my first year at the Ministry Training Center and had just learned about God using humans to heal other humans. For me, it gets even more interesting when I think about how that all happened.

I had NEVER done anything like that before. The fact that I just walked into that room, laid my hands on his chest, and commanded that rhythm to return to normal was not something I normally did. Where did I get the courage to do that? It was a gift, plain and simple. It was a gift of faith given to me from the Holy Spirit just for that moment.

Faith is a word that most Christians are and should be familiar with. All of us recognize that we used faith when we accepted Jesus as our Savior because Ephesians 2:8 tells us,

> "*We are saved by grace through faith.*"

We also learn in the book of Hebrews that "*without faith, it is impossible to please God.*" (Hebrews 11:6) These are all common examples of using our faith, but that's not the faith I'm talking about here.

I believe this gift of faith is something special that the Holy Spirit imparts to us for a short period of time to accomplish something we would not normally be able to accomplish. Listen, I sometimes struggle with my faith. Not the faith I have in Jesus Christ, but the faith that is necessary to bring heaven to earth. The faith necessary to set the captives free, and to bring healing to the hurting. I struggle with releasing faith in myself and putting my faith completely in God, and with understanding and waiting on God's timing. When He doesn't do things when I think He should, I try to make things happen on my own, WITHOUT HIM. At times, this can be a daily struggle for me and it demonstrates a lack of faith on my part.

THE HOLY SPIRIT DOLES OUT A PART OF GOD'S FAITH DIRECTLY TO THE BELIEVER TO ACCOMPLISH SOMETHING SUPERNATURAL.

The "gift of faith" is something completely different. It is not confined by doubts or unbelief, because it is faith of a divine nature. The Holy Spirit doles out a part of God's faith directly to the believer to accomplish something supernatural. Why? Because HE is supernatural! In Mark 11:23, Jesus tells us,

"For assuredly, I say to you, whoever says to this mountain, 'Be removed and be cast into the sea,' and does not doubt in his heart, but believes that those things he says will be done, he will have whatever he says."

Did you read that? It says WHOEVER! That means ANY believer can speak to the mountain and since I am a believer, that means me. There is no limitation to who is doing the speaking. The catch to this gift of faith is there cannot be any doubt. The Holy Spirit's divine faith drowns out the doubt and causes a miracle to happen.

Being the newbie Christian that I was, I would have never stepped forward to speak to that heart and command it to return to normal. This analytical mind could never comprehend that and would never allow me to put myself in a situation that would embarrass me. However, with the gift of faith imparted to me by the Holy Spirit, I was able to walk into the room and bring heaven to earth by bringing healing to a young man's heart.

I didn't stop to think about it. I didn't argue with the Holy Spirit telling Him, He had the wrong girl. I just walked in, laid my hands on his chest, commanded that heart to return to normal rhythm and when it did; I walked right back out. I was on cloud nine the rest of the day, of course! What an amazing God we have! One who would use the weakest of these to bring a supernatural touch from Himself to a young man who probably never even knew He was there.

****

Another exciting event that God allowed me to participate in, involved caring for a small two-month old baby. The baby presented to the emergency department with a fever of 103 degrees for about 24 hours. We get very concerned about fevers in young babies. Without a fully developed immune system to fight off infection, babies can get very sick, very quickly. Therefore, determining a source for the fever is vitally important. A myriad of tests had been run on the baby and they all returned inconclusive. We knew she had an infection of some sort, but we didn't know where. All that was left for us to do was a lumbar puncture to make sure the infection wasn't in her spinal fluid (meningitis), which could kill the baby quickly if not caught in time.

Lumbar punctures are not one of my favorite procedures, mostly because it involves sticking a very large needle into someone's back. I like it even less when we have to do it on a baby. Now, to add to the equation, the pediatrician on duty that day had not been very successful with pediatric lumbar punctures in the past. I couldn't imagine a worse scenario.

My job was to squish this baby into a tight ball that would leave her back curved and bulging towards the doctor. This doctor made two unsuccessful attempts as the baby cried hysterically.

Feverishly, she looked around the room for her parents or for anyone who could save her from her predicament. As the doctor prepared for his third attempt, there were tears in my eyes. To be honest, it took everything I had not to punch the doctor in his face! Thankfully, the Holy Spirit descended on the situation and spoke into my heart to begin praying in my heavenly language into the baby's ear. Within 30 seconds of quietly praying in her ear, the baby calmed down, enveloped in the Holy Spirit's peace. Guided by the Holy Spirit, the doctor was then able to perform the lumbar puncture successfully.

Your personal heavenly prayer language is different from your regular spoken language. It's a unique and special language that the Holy Spirit gives to you to help you change into the image of His only Begotten Son. With this prayer language, Holy Spirit gets directly involved with you in a prayer-relationship independent of anything else, including your mind. He already knows the plan that Father God has for you and pours it into you as you use your heavenly language, a language that is known by you and Him alone.

MIRACLES HAPPEN AND FAITH GROWS WHEN YOU USE YOUR HEAVENLY PRAYER LANGUAGE. He uses this language to pray for your calling, to implement the plan God has for your life, to edify you, and to charge you up with His Holy Power. His entire goal is to pull you out of everything Jesus set you free from and into everything Jesus promised you. Miracles happen and faith grows when you use your heavenly prayer language. I can tell you this, a miracle happened when that doctor successfully performed that lumbar puncture and MY faith grew a ton!

Whenever we our praying with the Holy Spirit, we are uttering divine secrets and spiritual laws. As we do this, the Holy Spirit brings everything into alignment with the purpose and plan God has for our lives. I believe there is an exchange of a supernatural origin when we pray using our heavenly prayer language. God trades our natural plans and ideas for His. Holy Spirit continually searches our hearts looking for anything that is against the will of God and gets rid of it (Romans 8:27), bringing us more into alignment with Him and His plans for our lives.

When we speak in a tongue that our mind does not recognize, our spirit is the part of us that is actually praying. That's why our mind/soul doesn't understand (See 1 Corinthians 14:2). Holy Spirit came in and created a new language with our spirit, giving us all power and authority of the Godhead. He prays the perfect prayer, a prayer that can only be understood and answered by God.

****

One afternoon, I received an order to give moderate sedation to an elderly patient for a procedure that she needed. We took her into the procedure room, moved her over onto the table, covered her with blankets, put oxygen on, and then I gave her a small touch of the sedation medications to help her relax and to see how she would respond to them. Five minutes later, another nurse came in to relieve me for my lunch break. I gave her report about the patient and everything I had done while in the room and left for my lunch break.

Upon my return, I found the patient out in the recovery area, in moderate respiratory distress, fighting for her life. I was terrified! What in the world happened after I left? Did I miss something or do something wrong? How did this happen? There was nothing left for me to do, so I just reached in and grabbed her hand. At that very moment, I felt her grab MY hand and she held on as if she was holding on for her dear life. I think she probably was. The situation resolved and she returned to her normal status and was taken back upstairs to her room.

However, the incident was far from over in my mind. I kept analyzing the chart, talking to the other nurses, and doctors, and techs, trying to wrap my mind around what had happened to that sweet lady. No one had any answers, yet I couldn't stop thinking about it. A few hours later, as I was driving from work to the training center for class, I found myself STILL trying to figure out what happened, until the Holy Spirit joined in the process and quietly answered my questions.

Unbeknownst to me, the patient had a condition known as COPD (Chronic Obstructive Pulmonary Disease). It's a disease where the airways in the lungs become blocked (or clogged) by either mucus or destruction of the airways. It's a slow progressing disease, but can be very challenging for the patient to breathe as the disease continues to progress. One of the key things in COPD is the patient stops responding to oxygen like healthy people. Excess supplemental oxygen actually causes them to stop breathing. I had put her on too much oxygen. I was at fault. My mistake could have cost the patient her life. THAT would have messed me up for a very long time. Thankfully, the Holy Spirit knew that.

He pointed out that I was also the reason that she survived.

I asked Him, "*How?*"

He said, "*Remember when you grabbed her hand.*"

I responded with, "*Yes, but how did that save her life? All I did was hold her hand!*"

He said, "*When you grabbed her hand, you made contact between the Spirit who lives inside of you (which is Me) and the Spirit who lived inside of her! When that contact was made, her spirit pulled on the life-giving Spirit in you. Because I'm a genius, I was able to resolve the issue quickly before something awful happened that you would never have forgiven yourself for. Therefore, she didn't die. That's how well I know you! I knew something like that would have tormented you. Because I love YOU (and her), she didn't die!*"

The Holy Spirit was able to use me to save this lady's life and I didn't have to do a thing but reach out and touch her. Why?

> "*You are of God, little children, and have overcome them, because He who is in you is greater than he who is in the world.*" ~ 1 John 4:4

What a great verse! Stop and read that again. Not only are we from God, but we are also overcomers! This is true, no matter the situation or circumstance. Why? Because the One Who NOW lives inside of us is greater than the one in the world. Imagine how much our lives could or better yet, WOULD change, if we ACTUALLY believed that one verse of scripture.

Let's take a moment to break that scripture down.

1. We are from God

2. We are overcomers

3. The One inside of us (Holy Spirit) is greater than the one (the devil) in the world

Now, that last part, "*The One inside of you is greater than the one in the world,*" indicates that there are two opposing forces in operation here.

1. The One inside of us (Holy Spirit)

2. The one in the world (the devil)

Think about it. If the Holy Spirit (or Jesus) lives inside of you, then:

1. Health and healing lives inside of you

2. Provision lives inside of you

3. Forgiveness lives inside of you

4. Mercy lives inside of you

5. Resurrection power lives inside of you

6. Supernatural power lives inside of you, and the list goes on.

Why? Because ANYTHING Holy Spirit is, including His nature AND character, lives inside of us. He is a life-producing Being! Everything He touches brings life! So when we reach out to touch someone, the Holy Spirit, Who resides in us, reaches out to touch the one we just touched. Since the Holy Spirit brings life, He produces life within our bodies and in everyone we come into contact with, because He is a life-producing God!

He is much greater than ANYTHING in this world. Therefore, sickness is no match for the health and healing that comes from the Holy Spirit. We can overcome sickness, whether it's attacking us or someone near us, because the Holy Spirit is greater! This is true for every area of our lives and for the lives of those we encounter on a daily basis.

WHEN WE FINALLY BELIEVE WHAT THE BIBLE SAYS, OUR RESPONSES TO LIFE AND THOSE AROUND US WILL CHANGE, ALLOWING THE HOLY SPIRIT TO BRING CHANGE INTO EVERYONE WE MEET.

In Acts 3, Peter and John didn't have any money to give to the beggar, but the life and healing of Jesus were living on the inside of them, so they could give that freely and therefore the beggar's legs were healed and He was able to walk. When we finally believe what the Bible says, our responses to life and those around us will change, allowing the Holy Spirit to bring change into everyone we meet. We have to believe and then understand that "*He Who lives insides of us is greater than he who is in the world.*" (1 John 4:4)

****

One afternoon a fifteen-year-old girl sat down in my triage chair, crying hysterically. Her dad and sister were with her. Dad reported that she had been crying like this for a week and he just didn't know how to help her. I could tell that it was tearing him apart.

Now, because of obvious reasons, I asked the father to step out so that I could ask the young girl a few sensitive questions without him being there. First, I asked her whether or not her father had hurt her in any way. Thankfully, her reply was "no" and by the father's previous response, I didn't think so either, but I wasn't willing to take any chances. Then, I asked her if she had been raped and/or abused by anyone else. Again, her answer was thankfully, "*No.*" Finally, I asked her if she had taken any drugs or consumed any alcohol, she denied that also. Three responses. Three correct answers. I could take a deep breath. There are only a few other situations that are worse than taking care of a child/teenager that has been abused and/or raped.

While I was talking with her, I noticed that she was wearing a cross necklace, so I asked her if she was a Christian. With tears in her eyes and mild sniffles, she replied, "*Yes,*" followed by a slight smile. So, I asked her if I could pray with her and she excitedly said, "*Yes!*" I asked her if I could lay my hands on her head and after giving me permission, she closed her eyes waiting to receive what God had for her.

Well, I am here to tell you, He had a LOT to give her! Thank You Jesus!

I took authority over the situation in the name of Jesus and by the Power of the Holy Spirit. I cast out the spirits of depression, oppression, and anxiety. She immediately stopped crying and sniffling. As I continued to pray a blessing over her, I could visibly see her demeanor change and her face relaxed and softened, as she let out a deep, releasing sigh. I completed the prayer by inviting the peace of Jesus to enter her heart.

She opened her eyes and gave me the biggest smile.

I asked her how she was feeling and she said, "*Much better. I don't feel that weight pushing down on me anymore, and I don't feel sad. Do I need to stay? I feel so much better!*" Unfortunately, because of her presentation, legally, she had to be thoroughly evaluated by an emergency physician before she could be released. It didn't matter. She was free and she knew it. There wasn't another tear during her entire visit and she amicably communicated with her dad and sister until she was discharged.

Her dad pulled me aside and asked me what happened to change her. I told him that his daughter gave me permission to pray for her and I just asked Jesus into the situation. Jesus knew exactly what was causing the problem and resolved it. Dad thanked me profusely as they walked out to their car.

She was a Christian and yet she was so blinded by the devil that she wasn't even able to ask Him for help. That's where the body of Christ comes in. We are to step in as ambassadors for the Lord Jesus Christ and facilitate an encounter with the One Who knows all things (1 John 3:20; Isaiah 40:28; Romans 11:33) and desires to heal ALL things (Psalm 103:3; Matthew 4:23, 9:35, 12:15; Acts 10:38). As we grow and mature in the things of God, we learn how to discern things. The more we use it, the stronger it becomes.

WHEN WE LAY HANDS ON SOMEONE OR PRAY IN THE SPIRIT FOR SOMEONE, WE ARE BRINGING THE SPIRITUAL REALITY INTO THE PHYSICAL REALM.

Ok, let me take a step back for just a moment. God created us in His image. He created us with a body, a soul, and a spirit (see 1 Thessalonians 5:23). We are three-part beings just like He is. Our bodies give us the right to exist on earth and communicate with the physical realm. Our spirits were made new when we were born again. Our souls make a way for the two parts of us to communicate with each other. When we lay hands on someone or pray in the spirit for someone, we are bringing our spiritual reality into the physical realm. That's what Jesus was saying in Matthew 6:10.

> *"Your kingdom come. Your will be done on earth as it is in heaven"*

He was instructing us on how important it is to bring heaven (or spiritual realms) into the physical realm in which we live. Our bodies were created to do that. Check out 1 Corinthians 6:19.

> *"Or do you not know that your body is the temple of the Holy Spirit Who is in you, Whom you have from God, and you are not your own?"*

So, if your body was created to house the Holy Spirit AND it was created to allow your spirit being to communicate with the physical realm, then how much more will the Holy Spirit who dwells inside of you, be able to communicate with the physical realm? As you partner with the Holy Spirit, spiritual realities like healing the sick through touch and receiving words of wisdom, knowledge, and/or prophecy can now be released by the Holy Spirit into the physical realm.

Now, in the same way that the Holy Spirit can influence us, other spirits who are not from the heavenly realm can also influence us. For example, if one minute you are fine and the next minute you are feeling afraid, you can bet that you have most likely encountered a spirit of fear. When that spirit of fear is nearby, it has the ability to activate a chemical cascade within your body that gives you the feeling of being afraid, but the source is actually spiritual. Anyone can sense that spirit of fear. It's what we do about it that matters. More often than not, we get into agreement with this feeling of fear and it continues to influence our mind, will, and emotions (also known as the soul), which ultimately influences our thoughts, actions, and behaviors.

The beautiful thing is, as we learn to hear the voice of Holy Spirit and spend more time with Him, we will begin to recognize those voices that are NOT from Him and we can deal with them as the Holy Spirit directs.

> Hebrews 5:14 says, *"But solid food belongs to those who are of full age, that is, those who by reason of use have their senses exercised to discern both good and evil."*

Ha! Did you see that? The more we use our spiritual senses, the better we will be able to discern good and evil. I love it when Holy Spirit speaks to me, even while I'm writing.

As we continue to learn and grow and use our ability to discern, Jesus removes our blindfolds (in the spirit realm) to sin and opens our eyes to see things as they really are. For instance, the world will just feel fear and not think much about it, while the more mature, spiritually in tune Christian will recognize that a spirit of fear is lurking nearby. Likewise, the rest of the world will feel peace and we will know that the Holy Spirit is actually present. You see, everyone senses the activity of the spirit realm, but not everyone is able to discern what is actually going on.

WHEN WE RECOGNIZE OUTSIDE INFLUENCES LIKE FEAR, DISCOURAGEMENT, ANGER, RAGE, OR DEPRESSION, ETC., WE CAN NOW CHOOSE NOT TO PARTNER WITH THAT SPIRIT.

When we recognize outside influences like fear, discouragement, anger, rage, or depression, etc., we can now choose not to partner with that spirit. We can effectively tell that spirit that we see them, we recognize them, and we can command them to leave, destroying their influence on us and/or the situation. THAT is what I did with the young girl in this story. I discerned the spirits that were affecting her and commanded them to leave, in Jesus' mighty name!

You can learn to do that, too! This gifting can develop so strongly within you that you will recognize those spirits before they even have the ability to influence you. But remember, the only way it can develop, is by spending time in the presence of the Holy Spirit, learning His voice, His ways, etc. Accept the fact that you are a spiritual being and you ARE spiritually sensitive. Start practicing discernment with Holy Spirit. As you do, you will become stronger and more able to bring heaven to earth!

****

One final example of encountering Holy Spirit in the ER occurred within the past year. I have been working on increasing the number of encounters my patients have with Holy Spirit while I am at work. On this particular morning, I prayed over Room #1, anointing it and claiming the room for Holy Spirit, and barring any evil spirits (aka demons) from entering the room; but once we got busy, I forgot all about it.

A certain man arrived in the ER via taxi from a local free clinic because they felt he was very confused and acting as if he might have had a stroke. During my triage, I have to ask a lot of questions to try to narrow down why the patient is seeking help in the ER. Throughout my questioning, not once did he stumble over the answers. His neurological exam was pristine. He was calm and cooperative, allowed me to perform all of the testing to rule out strokes, followed all commands, and even thanked me when we were finished. Since all of the testing came back within normal limits, we discharged him home.

His friend that was with him could not believe how different he was from the free clinic. I didn't think much about it until I was on my break. After finishing my meal, when possible, I like to spend some quiet time with God to ask about what has occurred so far and to prepare for the rest of the shift (this does not happen as often as it should, but it did on this day). He reminded me of how I anointed the room before the shift began and dedicated the room to Him. Because of that simple action, the spirits that were affecting that man were unable to manifest through him. You see, he was being tortured like the man in the tombs possessed by Legion (Mark 5:1-20), but when he entered Room #1, the spirits could not come in or they were bound. Either way, the man was able to function as himself for that brief period of time, something he probably had not been able to do for quite a while – ALL because of the authority that I hold because of Jesus Christ.

Listen, as Christians, we all know that Jesus died for our sins when He was crucified on that cross over 2000 years ago. His sacrifice is the key to healing, wholeness, and deliverance from the kingdom of darkness, but Jesus didn't stay dead! On the third day, the Holy Spirit entered that tomb and breathed life into Jesus' dead body, making Him brand new. He was changed so much that even His closest friends and disciples did not recognize Him (See Luke 24:16).

When you and I accept Jesus as our Lord and Savior and get into a supernatural partnership with Him, we too are changed! It's the process Christians like to refer to as being born again (John 3:3). One important thing we must realize is that Jesus didn't raise Himself from the dead. He couldn't. The Holy Spirit did it (Romans 8:11). The same thing applies to us. We can choose to die in Christ, but we cannot make ourselves new. It's the work of the Holy Spirit Who causes us to be born again.

> Romans 8:11 - *"But if the Spirit of Him who raised Jesus from the dead dwells in you, He who raised Christ from the dead will also give life to your mortal bodies through His Spirit who dwells in you."*

Just like Jesus, when you chose to accept Him as your Lord and Savior, you were made into a new creation (2 Corinthians 5:17). Now you can freely claim the words Paul wrote.

[76]

Galatians 2:20 - *"I have been crucified with Christ; it is no longer I who live, but Christ lives in me; and the life which I now live in the flesh I live by faith in the Son of God, who loved me and gave Himself for me."*

So, we're a new creation. Now what? Why don't we notice a change? Why do we continue to live our lives, making the same mistakes, committing the same sins over and over? It's because most Christians stop here. They try to live their lives like Jesus did 2000 years ago. What do I mean by that? Jesus didn't stay there. He didn't continue to walk on this earth. Instead, He ascended to the right hand of the Father with all of His rights, power, authority, and intimacy with the Father.

Now here's where it gets really exciting! If we died with Jesus and we rose from that death with Jesus and were made into a new creation just like Jesus, then it goes without saying that we have ascended with Jesus to the right hand of the Father! It tells us that in the Bible. Check it out for yourself!

4 "But God, who is rich in mercy, because of His great love with which He loved us, 5 even when we were dead in trespasses, made us alive together with Christ (by grace you have been saved), 6 and raised us up together, and made us sit together in the heavenly places in Christ Jesus" ~ Ephesians 2:4-6

As a disciple and follower of the Lord, Jesus Christ, we have been invited to reign with Him from the right hand of the Father. We have been granted access to all His power, all His authority, and all of His intimacy with the Father.

To the one who is victorious, I will give the right to sit with me on my throne, just as I was victorious and sat down with my Father on his throne ~ Revelations 3:21

So, let me ask you a question. Are you still struggling with sin in your life? Do you feel like you are circling the same mistakes over and over? Perhaps it's because you really haven't put your faith in the Lord, Jesus Christ. Look, I'm not pointing fingers here, but if your life hasn't changed, then you are missing something truly amazing.

> 1 John 5:18 - *"We know that whoever is born of God does not sin; but he who has been born of God keeps himself, and the wicked one does not touch him."*

When a Christian tries to tell me that sin is inevitable, it shows me that they have not accepted the freedom that Jesus paid for on the cross. Will we mess up? Will we make mistakes? Of course we will, but when we do, Holy Spirit convicts us, we repent, and then we are free. The sin I'm referring to is that willful desire to do something that we know is wrong. Something that is completely against the will of the Father. THAT desire doesn't exist in me anymore.

If you are stuck in the life that you have always lived — still living in sin — it's time to fully trust the Holy Spirit. Receive the forgiveness that Jesus has made freely available to us at the cross and through His resurrection! Admit that when Jesus died, you died. Embrace the sacrifice of Jesus, and ask the Holy Spirit to make you a new creation. Ask the Holy Spirit to help you overcome even the temptation of that sin. Then and only then, will you be able to walk around in the authority that Jesus has freely given you.

As I sat and pondered the stories in this particular chapter, I wondered how I would tie all of them together with what I feel Holy Spirit is trying to teach through this book. My heart was filled with emotions as I realized that when the light of God shines through one of His children, it draws people who are searching for hope and purpose. Each story in this chapter is a small representation of the lives of five of His children, all bound and searching for Him. Because of my obedience and understanding of this part of the gospel, these five children in particular, were given the opportunity to experience His love in one form or another.

I have the immense privilege of watching God touch His children's lives through me. When you are transformed by God, you become a light in the darkness, and people everywhere are drawn to you. It's an incredible experience to be used as a tool in the hand of the Most High God.

Chapter Ten

Out of the Box

"He sent His Word and healed them..." ~ Psalm 107:20

One day, a few years ago, I received this email from my friend who is a missionary in Narnia.

Hey Rach!
Need your prayers. I have had giardia for two weeks and am tired out by it!
Thanks!
Mich

Here was my reply.

But of course, my dear sister! It is an honor to pray for you!!!

Jesus said, if we would speak to a mountain in our lives and tell it to be plucked up and thrown into the sea, it would have to obey us (Mark 11:23-24). So, because Jesus said to do it, and because we are obedient to His commands; let's speak to the mountain of giardia in your life!

GIARDIA, LISTEN UP AND PAY ATTENTION. WE ARE TALKING TO YOU! IN THE NAME OF JESUS CHRIST, THE ANOINTED ONE. I COMMAND YOU TO BE PLUCKED UP AND THROWN OUT OF MICHELLE'S LIFE AND BODY. YOU HAVE NO CHOICE. YOU CAN'T STAY. YOU HAVE TO LEAVE. THERE IS NO ALTERNATIVE, NO OTHER OPTION. PACK YOUR BAGS, HIT THE ROAD, AND DON'T COME BACK ANYMORE.

Today's mountain is tomorrow's testimony, Michelle! YEAH! It doesn't matter how big the mountain is, and it doesn't matter how long the mountain has been there. What does matter is what Jesus says about the mountain; it HAS to obey us. The mountain of giardia has been eradicated and eliminated from your body and from your life. You are healed, healthy, and whole in the mighty name of Jesus!

I proclaim healing for your body. By Jesus' stripes, you were healed. The healing, life-giving, disease-destroying power of God is working in your body. It drives out ALL manner of sickness and disease. You are full of life, health, strength, and vitality. You are healthy and whole from the top of your head to the soles of your feet. Every organ in your body operates and functions the way God created it, without disease or malfunctions, especially your gastrointestinal tract. EVERY system in your body operates and functions with supernatural efficiency. Your nervous system, lymphatic system, DIGESTIVE system, electrical system, circulatory system, and every other system, all function with 100 percent efficiency.

Jesus Himself bore your sickness and carried your disease; therefore, sickness and disease are not allowed to exist in your body. Your body is free from bacteria, viruses, growths, tumors, or obstructions of any kind.

The divine zoe life of God flows through you, quickening and making alive your mortal body. Your body is free from pain, discomfort, distress, and all symptoms of sickness. God's word is medicine to your flesh. You are not moved by how you feel, how you look, or any negative reports, because you believe God's Word and His word says YOU ARE HEALED! In the mighty name of Jesus Christ, YOU ARE HEALED! AMEN!

Love you!

PS: Some supporting scriptures that you probably ALREADY know, but are good reminders: Isaiah 53:4-5, Proverbs 4:20-22, Psalm 107:20, Matthew 8:17, 1 Peter 2:24.

Wow! As I read back over that email, I thought, "that was some pretty heavy stuff!" I was amazed at how authoritative I sounded. That HAD to be the Holy Spirit ministering to her THROUGH me! At that time in my life, I barely understood anything God had to say about healing.

Her reply confirms her healing.

THANK YOU, sister!
I have to say, that within 24 hours of this e-mail, I was TOTALLY healed! Really! I feel amazing now and am so glad that is over! Love you and I THANK GOD FOR YOU!

I learned so much from that brief email exchange between my friend and me.

1. How much the Holy Spirit wants to support His servants.

2. How much Holy Spirit can do through us if,... we will just step out in faith and let Him do the work.

3. How healing can even happen through email! Don't EVER hinder the Holy Spirit by limiting Him to what YOU think is possible!

On yet another occasion, while I was in Pennsylvania visiting my parents, I saw a post on Facebook from a friend telling everyone that her husband, who just happened to be the man who baptized me (Mark), was in the emergency room with an irregular heartbeat. Being the ER nurse that I am, I became very concerned and texted my friend to find out what was going on and if there was anything I could do.

Her response? "*Just pray! PLEASE!*"

So, that's exactly what I did. I went to Holy Spirit to find out why a young, healthy man would be exhibiting an irregular heartbeat. He, immediately gave me a picture of my friend Mark, lying in a hospital bed, with a distressed look on his face. What I saw next really grabbed my attention. On his chest, I saw a little black creature, about 6-8 inches tall in the shape of a teardrop with long arms and short legs. It was laughing and giggling hysterically as it kept reaching his hands in through Mark's chest and shaking them (his hands) all around. He would stop for a few seconds and then he would go right back at it. I immediately asked the Holy Spirit to clarify what I was seeing. He confirmed what I saw and encouraged me to use my authority to get rid of that thing. So, I said, "*In the name of Jesus Christ and by the power of the Holy Spirit, I command this agitating spirit to leave at once. This is a child of God and YOU are trespassing on sacred ground!*"

I kicked the creature and Poof! He was gone.

Not telling her what I had just experienced, I then texted his wife and asked her how he was doing. She reported that he was much calmer now. His heart rate had slowed down some, but it was still irregular and she was getting more concerned.

Holy Spirit told me to tell her that since she and her husband were now one, she could lay her head down on his chest and she would be able to bring his heart rate into rhythm with hers. Wow! There was no doubting that this advice could not have come from me. It was confirmed an hour or so later when she texted me to let me know that Mark's heart rhythm had converted back to a normal sinus rhythm and was pumping at a normal rate of 80. Glory to God!

Both of the stories I just shared are incredible and may be difficult to believe. They were difficult for ME to believe and they HAPPENED to and/or through me. Whether you choose to believe them or not doesn't change the fact that they happened - just like all of the other stories I've shared in this book. Holy Spirit is real and He is moving throughout the earth whenever we allow Him to. It's important to understand that He WANTS to heal you, today!

How often do we, as Christians prevent the movement of the Holy Spirit by limiting His flow to how WE think He should flow. Then, we wonder why our prayers feel like they never make it past the ceiling. We "try" to control the Holy Spirit and tell Him how to act or behave because we don't have enough faith. Oh no, it couldn't be OUR fault, could it? We limit Him, the Creator of the Universe, with our unbelief.

WE LIMIT HIM, THE CREATOR OF THE UNIVERSE, WITH OUR UNBELIEF.

As humans, we ALL try to keep Holy Spirit in a box. Some of our boxes are bigger than others, but we all have a box marked for God. Basically, we limit what He can or can't do or even what He will or won't do. Why can't we comprehend that He, the Creator of the Universe has given us ALL power in the world to accomplish ANYTHING?

The Bible clearly tells us that we can move mountains with just a tiny amount of faith (Matthew 17:20; Mark 11:23), so why aren't we? It also tells us in Philippians 4:13 that *"we can do ALL things through Christ who strengthens us."* All means ALL. So, why aren't we doing ALL things? I think it's because we really don't believe what God is telling us in the Bible, which really means we are calling God a liar. Although, He clearly says to us in Titus 1:2 that He CANNOT lie. In John 8:44, He tells us that the devil is the father of all lies. If we really believed what He said in the Bible, we would not be afraid to share our faith. We would want to shout ALL that He has done for us from the mountaintops. We would want everyone to know.

So, let me ask you a question. Do you only have enough faith to believe in salvation? Think about that! Is God/Jesus/Holy Spirit limited to your salvation only? Are you worried about being called a Jesus freak? Is that what you want to control your life?

We need to see the Word of God as the TRUTH that it is! We need to exercise your faith like a muscle and watch it grow. We need to believe that **ALL THINGS ARE POSSIBLE** (Job 42:2; Jeremiah 32:17; Matthew 19:26; Mark 9:23, 10:27; Luke 1:37, 18:27)! Meditate on these scriptures and GET a revelation of this truth. Our lives have four purposes.

1. To love God with all our hearts, and all our soul, and all our strength

2. To glorify the Creator of the Universe

3. To spread the good news

4. To build the Kingdom of heaven

Listen, we ALL put God in a box in EVERY area of our lives. You can say that you don't, but if you take a real honest look at yourself and your life, you will realize that you do. We pray prayers that are half faith and half doubt, which cancel each other out. So, how do we let God out of the box?

First, we have to take a good hard look at ourselves and realize that we cannot accomplish ANYTHING without Him. Nothing! We have to believe that NOTHING is IMPOSSIBLE with God. NOTHING! I don't know if you know this or not, but doubt and unbelief do not come from God. If they don't come from God, then they must come from our enemy, the devil, and he loves it when we limit Holy Spirit with our doubts. When we wallow in our doubts, we are actually believing the lies of the devil. God is truth! He does not function surrounded by lies.

Secondly, we HAVE to renew our minds. Romans 12:2 tells us to not be like this world and all of its lies and doubts, but to believe the Word of God so it will transform us. When that happens, when the lies and doubts are removed, there will be no confusion. We will know the perfect will of God for our lives!

So, let's start proclaiming the true greatness of our Creator! Let's let Him roam freely in our lives, and JUST WATCH in amazement at the wonders He can and will do for us.

Do you want miracles in your life? Do you want freedom and power that you never imagined possible? Do you want the enemy bound in chains, instead of you being bound in chains? Take God OUT OF THE BOX! Stop the doubting and the half-hearted prayers, rebuke the lies and doubt. Proclaim that the Creator of this universe has all the power, all the glory, and all the wonder we could ever want, need, or desire. He CAN and WILL do amazing things for and through us, but we have to let Him out of the box!

PROCLAIM THAT THE CREATOR OF THIS UNIVERSE HAS ALL THE POWER, ALL THE GLORY, AND ALL THE WONDER WE COULD EVER WANT, NEED, OR DESIRE.

Chapter Eleven

Father's Heart

"For I know the thoughts that I think toward you, says the Lord, thoughts of peace and not of evil, to give you a future and a hope." ~ Jeremiah 29:11

My church, Living Faith Church, used to offer a wonderful class known as Father's Heart. The class was absolutely amazing and life changing. It was a three-day class that ended with personal time with God and a time of ministry with Pastor Rob and his wife Michelle, the leaders of the course, speaking into each student's life.

During our quiet time at the end of the class, I chose to journal what I was feeling and thinking. I spent quite a bit of time complaining to God in my journal. You see, I had extremely high expectations of God when I signed up for this class. Don't get me wrong, I really enjoyed the class and learned so much, but I was expecting a life-changing moment at some point; but here we were at the end of the class and I had not had THE experience I was expecting. The words I wrote are not important. It was the words He spoke to me that I want to share with you.

He started by asking me, "*Are you done, yet? Can I speak?*" (Father God and I just have that type of relationship!) "*Of course, Father God,*" I replied.

He continued, "*Don't fear what I am going to say to you, Rachel. I have such amazing plans for you! I am so glad you came to this seminar so I could finally release you from the chains that have been binding you. You are going to experience a freedom you* have never known before. You are going to experience a love that you have never known before; you are going to experience a relationship with me and others that you have never known before! I am going to take you to new heights that are going to amaze you! Your relationships are going places that will surprise you."

"*Consider today as a new birth because a new creation will be exiting the building today. Don't go into condemnation over what I just said. There were issues before that were holding you back from who I created you to be, issues that you weren't even aware of before, but today, I have dealt with them, once and for all! They will hinder you no more!*"

"*Freedom is here to stay,*" He continued. "*Your new creation is being released for all of the world to see. EVERYONE will notice and wonder what happened. YOU will notice and KNOW what happened* → *you had an experience with Me, your Father!*"

"*Oh, how I love you! Oh, how I LOVE you, my beautiful child, my beautiful daughter -- the amazing woman I created you to be -- COME FORTH! Step out into this new life that I have for you. I am so proud of what you have already accomplished* → *but it is small potatoes compared to where you are going* → *where I am taking you! I have such big plans for you! And I don't use those words lightly -* **BIG PLANS!**"

"*Don't doubt. Don't question. Just follow my guidance. Touch who I tell you to touch. Hug who I tell you to hug. Pray for who I tell you to pray for. I am so excited for what is in store! You, only YOU, can accomplish what I have for you to accomplish. Don't be overwhelmed. Just wait for me. I will guide you and take you through each step and I will be there every step of the way. Music, writing, healing, teaching... The lives you are going to touch...*"

"*Yes, even prophesying and seeing into other's lives, just like Michelle just saw into yours!*"

At this point, I was feeling so overwhelmed and so unworthy.

Father God picked right up on that and continued further, "*My darling daughter, you will not be asked to do any of this alone. I will be with you through* **EVERYTHING!** *Look for me and I will be there. Call out to me and I will be there. I will NEVER leave you nor forsake you! You will have earthly help as well.*"

I responded with, "*I have so many questions.*"

He laughed and said, "*I know you do, but just be with Me and each question will be answered in its time. We are going on a journey, Rachel. It's going to be fun and exciting! Are you ready?*"

"*With You, Father, I am ready! Let's go!*"

You see, our conversations with God should flow easily, just like a conversation you would have with another person.   It's definitely NOT one-sided with us doing all the talking and presenting Him with our "Christmas list of needs". It's interaction! It's fun! It's alive! Is that how you would describe your prayer life or intimate times with the Lord? If not, they should be.

But I digress...

As I read through this journal entry, I noticed that Father God was talking to me, yet again, about my identity and who He made me to be. There is no earthly way I could accomplish anything He said in this journal entry. However, the person God saw and still sees today is far different from the person I had been seeing.

Heaven strongly desires for us to figure out who we are so the Holy Spirit can effectively use us to bring His kingdom here to the earth. Holy Spirit is anxiously waiting to release things in our lives, but He is hindered because we don't know who we are or even that Father God loves us.

AUTHORITY IN THE KINGDOM OF GOD IS BASED ON OUR UNDERSTANDING OF WHO WE ARE.

All of my life, I have been believing the lies that hell wants me to believe about myself. Hell doesn't want us to know who we are or even Whose we are. When we finally get a revelation on these very topics, we will walk in the supernatural authority and power that has already been given to us. Authority in the kingdom of God is based on our understanding of who we are.

Most believers don't walk in a portion of their identity as sons and daughters of the Most High God because they still believe they are servants, but Jesus told us in John 15:15 that we are no longer servants.

> *"I no longer call you servants, because a servant does not know his master's business. Instead, I have called you friends, for everything that I learned from my Father, I have made known to you."* ~ John 15:15

HAVE YOU EVER MEDITATED ON THE FACT THAT AS A DISCIPLE OF THE LORD JESUS CHRIST, YOU ARE NO LONGER A SERVANT, BUT A FRIEND OF GOD?

As I continue to gain an understanding of this revelation for myself, I am realizing what a powerful key it is to my identity. What an awesome privilege it is to be a friend of God and to no longer be a servant! Have you ever meditated on the fact that as a disciple of the Lord Jesus Christ, YOU are no longer a servant, but a friend of God? Take a few minutes right now to think about that. Read John 15:15 over and over and ask Holy Spirit to reveal to you what is really being said there. I promise you, it will ROCK YOUR WORLD!

After you have spent some quality time on John 15:15, move on over to Galatians 4:7 and spend some time there.

> "*So you are no longer a slave but a son; and since you are a son, God has also made you an heir.*" ~ Galatians 4:7

WE are sons & daughters of the King, which means, according to Galatians 4:7, we inherit EVERYTHING that Jesus died for us to have.

- His power
- His glory
- His justice
- His mercy
- His compassion
- His joy
- His peace
- His love
- His healing
- His prosperity
- His freedom
- His EVERYTHING!

Thankfully, Jesus didn't just die - He was resurrected and sits at the right hand of the Father. Then, He sent His Holy Spirit to live inside of us, so He can work through us. He couldn't do any of that if we were still servants. He has given us amazing access to ALL the resources of heaven - everything listed above and so much more, as part of our inheritance.

As I ponder those two verses, it brings peace, comfort, and excitement to me as I think about the things God has revealed to me through my journal. No longer do I feel overwhelmed or incapable of accomplishing the things He has called me to do. I am a friend of the Most High God. I am a daughter of the Most High God! I have access to all the resources of my Father's kingdom and do you know what the best part is? HE LIVES INSIDE OF ME and will accomplish His plan for my life and the lives of everyone I come into contact with.

As Believers, we are no longer slaves; we are sons and daughters of the Most High God. We have access to angels! We have access to the Holy Spirit and His dunamis power! No longer should we be content to live an ineffectual Christian life. Instead, we should be excited to lay hands on the sick and watch them recover, cleanse lepers, cast out demons, change weather systems, and even raise people from the dead (Mark 15:16-18). We should be excited to allow God to do whatever He chooses to do through us. God's Holy Spirit lives in us so that He can work miracles through us, just like He did through Jesus. This is my identity, and this is YOUR identity, as a Believer in the Lord, Jesus Christ.

Christians have the power and ability to bring their beliefs, true or not, into a natural existence. For example, if a Believer does not believe that the Holy Spirit will use them to heal others, then their faith in that lie will make it their reality. They won't pray for the sick, nor seek out opportunities to learn about praying for the sick. If they are called upon to pray for someone, their faith in that lie, will prevent the person they are praying for from receiving any healing through them. Therefore, perpetuating the lie and making it even more a part of their reality. Once we accept a false identity about ourselves, we build re-enforcements (also known as strongholds) to keep that lie protected, thus making it our reality.

"Oh, I prayed for someone once and they still died. God doesn't heal the sick through me."

As long as you believe that, God will NEVER heal anyone through you. It's really that simple. Your mind is incapable of recognizing a lie. That's a fact. God will not heal through you while you are believing that lie. God values your will above everything else. However, the truth is that God heals through His children. He's just waiting for us to step up, refute the lie, and claim our inheritance. We need to shout, "*No, It's not okay that people aren't healed through me when I pray for them. I'm a believer and most importantly, a child of the MOST HIGH GOD! Jesus healed the sick, so I will heal the sick because He lives inside of me!"*

So, what do you have faith in?

      1. The lie that God will not heal through you or

      2. The truth that God **DOES** heal through you?

Which one do you think requires more faith? Think about that. If I believe that the person I am praying for will be healed, then God's power to heal is present to empower my faith! However, the opposite is also true. If I believe that God would NEVER use me to heal the sick, that will also become reality because my faith will empower that lie.

If we want to walk in God's power, experiencing His miracles, signs, and wonders, we just need to believe that we can. We need to believe EVERY promise that is in the Bible and then ACT on it! Act as if it has already happened! It's this kind of faith that moves mountains, changes atmospheres, heals the sick, casts out demons, and raises the dead!

Chapter Twelve

Visions During Worship

"God is Spirit, and those who worship Him must worship in spirit and truth." ~ John 4:24

Praise and worship is the most active time for me to encounter the Holy Spirit. I learned a lot about praise and worship in the Ministry Training Center at Living Faith Church - what it's supposed to look like and be like for me. To be honest, it was very difficult for me in the beginning. I thought it was supposed to be a certain way for every person, but it's not. It's a time with you and Holy Spirit and anything can happen during YOUR time with Him. For me, it's NEVER the same. Sometimes we just talk, other times He shows me a picture or puts an impression in my heart.

My favorite communication is when He creates a picture and puts me right in the middle of it. The first time He did that with me was during worship in the Ministry Training Center. We had worship every day before class for 30-45 minutes. It really opened the realm of the Spirit and opened my heart to receive what the Holy Spirit had for me that day. On this particular day, I really entered into an amazing time with Him. I was standing there, wanting to feel Him. My heart was locked in. Suddenly, He was there with me.

He whispered to me, "*I just love your heart! Will you give it to Me?*"

"*Absolutely,*" I said. "*Please! Just take it!*"

He smiled at me and His eyes were so filled with love as He reached into my chest and took hold of my heart. As soon as His hands were firmly wrapped around my heart, the shell of my body just fell to the ground. All that was left... was my heart.

"*This is who you REALLY are, Rachel,*" He said to me. "*This, right here, this heart in my hand, is who you REALLY are. I want you to remember, THIS is how I see you. I know your heart. The rest of that body is temporary and does not define you. So, stop allowing it to define who you are!*"

He wasn't yelling. He spoke very gently. I included the exclamation point because I felt HIS heart as He spoke to me. Never have I felt such warmth and love before. It was really life changing to receive such a revelation. Jesus knows my heart and likes to spend time there! He also knows that this human body is just a vessel that allows me to communicate with this natural world. It's NOT who I am, and it's definitely not who I want to be.

You may think that was a nice picture or I could have "imagined it". Let me tell you, when you receive revelation from the Holy Spirit, you know, that you Know, that you KNOW, it is from Him! The experience is more real than anything you experience in the natural and you can't deny it! It changes you at the core of who you are.

Another vivid picture I had with Jesus during worship in the training center happened while we were singing a song about jumping into the river. I decided I was going to do just that -- I "jumped in the river". There was no wading or testing the temperature of the water with my toe, I just jumped right in - Ker SPLASH!

In the beginning, I was just swimming around, enjoying the water and the freedom of swimming around and I heard Jesus say, "*I want you to go deeper. GO DEEPER!*"

So, I did just that. I dove deeper. The deeper I went, the more challenging it became, but when I would stop striving, I would just drop, deeper and deeper. The Lord spoke to me and said,

"THAT is an example of going deeper with me. The more you try, the harder it will be. When you allow ME to take you deeper, there won't be any need for striving or struggling on your part. Just be with Me and I will take you to depths that you didn't even know existed. Just be with Me! Spend time with Me! Worship Me!"

Worship time was ending, but I found myself not wanting to come up from the deep end of the pool. I would have been content to stay there forever. The amazing thing though, is we can go there anytime we want and spend as much time there as we want. We just have to want it. I had to ask myself, *"How much do I want it? How much do I want to spend my time at the deep end of the pool with Jesus?"* It's easy to get caught up in the struggles of the day. It should be EVEN easier to go to the deep end of the pool, because Jesus does all of the work!

So, who's going to join me in the deep end of the pool? Who wants REAL and AUTHENTIC worship with the God of the Universe? Who's tired of <u>pretending</u> to spend time in HIS presence?

WHAT MAKES WORSHIP REAL, AUTHENTIC, AND PURE IS NOT OUR SURROUNDINGS, BUT THE INTENT OF OUR HEART.

What makes worship real, authentic, and pure is not our surroundings, but the intent of our heart. It's that moment when our struggling hearts make it outside of the walls that we created to protect ourselves and actually bring honor and praise to the ONLY One Who is worthy to receive it! When it flows from a true, sincere heart, even a small amount of praise becomes powerful and holy!

How many of you view worship as a duty, something you do because some Sunday school teacher or pastor said it was important? Don't get me wrong, obedience is extremely important, but how many of you would be happy if your loved ones only came to visit you because they were told to or because they felt obligated? I'm pretty sure that would be NONE of you and neither would I. I don't believe God wants that either.

How can we develop an intimate relationship with Him, if we only spend time with Him so we can grow? How much more meaningful would that quality time be if both parties chose to be there because they enjoyed each other's company? THAT, my friends, is where real and authentic worship comes from -- it flows from the heart of the one who is worshipping.

So, what is worship? It's showing God how much we love and adore Him. It really IS that simple.

So, how do we get there? How do we love God, especially if we have never had an intimate relationship with Him? We make this so difficult. I know I did, but we need to remember that the Gospel is simple! The key to loving God through worship is found in 1 John 4:19.

> "*We love Him because He first loved us.*"

It really IS THAT SIMPLE! The more we understand HOW MUCH He loves us, the more we are able to love Him in return. We NEED to get a revelation on how much He loves us. Our ability to love Him is limited by our understanding of His love for us. THIS is not a human concept. This is not an earthly concept. It is an indisputable law of the

THE MORE WE UNDERSTAND HOW MUCH HE LOVES US, THE MORE WE ARE ABLE TO LOVE HIM IN RETURN.

Kingdom of God, similar to the natural law of gravity. It's truth on a spiritual level. Do you know that you are loved by the Father, the Son, and the Holy Spirit? If you do, then you have the ability to love Them in return.

If you don't know this simple truth, that the Father, the Son, and the Holy Spirit ALL love you, then you are not capable of loving Them, and therefore, are unable to worship Them. If you do not recognize Their love for you, then your worship will be mixed with hidden purposes and agendas. Do you know that before you even THOUGHT of worshipping God, He ALREADY loved you perfectly? If you are worshiping Him out of duty and/or obligation, you have missed the point. **Real and authentic worship must be relationship-based.**

God made us, so He could love us. God CHOSE to spend time with Adam and Eve in the garden. He didn't instruct them to build a church where they could go and sing songs about Him, celebrate with one-sided conversations, and learn about Him from others who didn't really know Him. He spent time with them because He loved them - pure and simple. He loved walking in the cool of the morning with them, sharing His heart, and loving them in His way, but then tragedy occurred.

Eve was deceived and Adam sinned. Not only did Adam and Eve's bodies begin to die, but the relationship between them and God was severed - their intimacy was gone. Duty and obligation replaced an intimate, eternal relationship of real and authentic love.

Thankfully, the story doesn't end there. God, the Father, sent His one and only Begotten Son to pay the price for our sins. We now have the ability to develop a real and authentic relationship with the One Who created us. He is revealing Himself to our hearts. Showing us His nature, His desires, and Who He is. Paul preached about this in Ephesians.

> "*That the God of our Lord Jesus Christ, the Father of glory, may give to you the spirit of wisdom and revelation*

IN THE KNOWLEDGE OF HIM' ~ Ephesians 1:17 (also see Ephesians 1:18)

WHEN TRUE KNOWLEDGE OF WHO HE IS IS RESTORED, TRUE WORSHIPPERS WILL COME FORTH.

When true knowledge of Who He is is restored, true worshippers will come forth. When we begin our journey into relationship with God, our views of Him are very limited. Our worship is based on our understanding of Who He is - which is really no understanding at all. However, the more time we spend with Him, learning about Who He is, and what He wants; then and only then, will our worship to Him become real and authentic.

It's in those intimate times with the Father that we begin to see how REAL and AUTHENTIC He has been with us. He begins to share the gazillion good thoughts He has for us and about us. Don't believe that God has good thoughts about you? Take a look at Psalm 139:17-18:

> **17** *"How precious also are Your thoughts to me, O God! How great is the sum of them!* **18** *If I should count them, they would be more in number than the sand; when I awake, I am still with You."*

The only conclusion I can come to concerning that scripture is I am loved. We are loved by Father God, Jesus, and the Holy Spirit. WE are loved by Them, so much, that we will NEVER be able to understand the depths of Their love for us! Catch hold of this truth, and I promise, your life will NEVER be the same! Remember, you can love God because He loved YOU first! Real and authentic worship is just YOUR response to His love.

So, how do we learn how to love God, this infinite Being, who makes something great out of something so small and weak? Most Christians go through life with very wrong ideas of Who God is. We see others "being blessed" and wonder how this God, Who loves us all the same, could bless them and not us! We then develop a false understanding that maybe God isn't really that good after all. We turn our circumstances and disappointments into some kind of measurement of how much God really loves or DOESN'T love us. Come on! We have ALL been there at one point or another in our lives - determining in our minds and hearts who God must be, according to how life has treated us.

Let's get real here. God is good ALL THE TIME! God is Love ALL the time! What's NOT to love? What's NOT to worship? This is what we need to understand, because when we do, we will willingly and easily drop at His feet, in awe of all that He is, humbled by His glory, and amazed by His beauty. Worship is the result of our personal relationship with the Father. Real and authentic worship requires me to have a revelation of how God sees me, an understanding of my true identity, and how much I am loved. From that knowledge, I am able AND willing to respond to that love. We love because He first loved us (1 John 4:19)! It's really that simple.

Chapter Thirteen

Words of Knowledge

"But the manifestation of the Spirit is given to each one for the profit of all: for one is given the word of wisdom, through the Spirit, to another the word of knowledge through the same Spirit, to another the gift of faith by the same Spirit, to another gifts of healings by the same Spirit..." ~ 1 Corinthians 12:7-10

It was during my second year at the Ministry Training Center that I had the privilege of being taught by Bebette. At the time, the class she was teaching (Spiritual Dimensions) was the toughest class for me by far! Not because she was a difficult teacher, but because the material was very new to me, and my analytical mind had an extremely difficult time wrapping itself around this teaching.

One evening during class, we spent a lot of time praying in the spirit and just soaking in the Presence of God. Afterwards, Bebette went around the class and asked anyone if they wanted to share what Father God had revealed to them during this time. Almost everyone in the class shared, but me. Everyone else's experiences seemed (to me) to be positive and uplifting, but mine wasn't! God was convicting me and it struck me at the core.

He revealed to me that I was carrying a lot of un-forgiveness towards my classmates.

"*MY classmates, Lord? Really?*" I said.

"*Yes, Rachel,*" He replied. "*You are harboring un-forgiveness towards them for not meeting your expectations."* What expectations you might ask? Well, I will tell you. From the first day of classes, I had always believed that I was the spiritual baby of the group. I believed that everyone was so much further than I was, because EVERYTHING I was learning in the Training Center was so new to me. THAT was a LIE straight from the pit of hell, but I believed it! I expected my classmates to share more of their "Advanced" spirituality I thought they had. When they didn't, I developed unforgiveness towards each one of them because I believed they were holding something back from me.

How in the world was I going to share THAT in class?

Since I couldn't figure out how to do that, I did what I thought was the next best thing. As soon as the first hour of class was over and we took a break, I ran! Yes, I did! I packed up all my books, notebooks, and Bible and I went straight to my car and drove home.

As childish and/or immature as that may seem, it was where I was. However, something amazing came from that experience. It was the first time in my life that I didn't pick up the phone to call someone. This time, I ran to Father God. I screamed! I cried! I apologized and repented and then I cried some more; and God was there. He gathered my wounded pride and damaged heart up onto His lap and He just loved on me, speaking soft words of forgiveness and love. This was a learning moment and it brought me straight to Him, right where He wanted me to be.

That was a Thursday evening. I spent the rest of the weekend secluded in my room with Him. We talked about so many things, mostly about the plans He had for me and places He was taking me. He also shared with me where each of my classmates were in their relationship with Him. He gave me a word that I could share with each one of them, individually, as well as a word for the class as a whole. It was an incredible time of just being with Him, learning and growing, giving and receiving. Sadly, I didn't journal any of it and I had forgotten how truly special that time was until Holy Spirit brought it back to my remembrance as I have been writing this book.

Encountering Holy Spirit on such an intimate level should be something we do on a daily basis instead of from time to time. Sharing these encounters with you is reminding me of the intimate, special relationship that I share with Him.

After receiving these words for my classmates from Holy Spirit, I met with Bebette to discuss what had happened and how Jesus had given me those words. Then, I shared the corporate word I had received for the class with her. She confirmed that I had definitely heard from the Lord and she wanted me to share it with the class.

Wait! What? Share it with the class? Is she kidding? I don't think so!

Nope! She was not kidding. The corporate word for the class went right along with the teaching she shared with us that day. I even shared each individual word with the class and most of my classmates later told me that was exactly what they needed to hear, or it was an exact answer to a prayer that was in their heart.

Wow! Encountering the Holy Spirit is absolutely incredible! You should try it sometime.

Ok. So, what are these "words" (words of knowledge) that I've been talking about?

The Bible talks about words of knowledge in Paul's letter to the church in Corinth.

> *7 "But the manifestation of the Spirit is given to each one for the profit of all: 8 for one is given the word of wisdom, through the Spirit, to another the word of knowledge through the same Spirit, 9 to another the gift of faith by*

the same Spirit. To another gifts of healings by the same Spirit, **10** *to another the working of miracles, to another different kinds of tongues, to another the interpretation of tongues.* **11** *But one and the same Spirit works all these things, distributing to each one individually as He wills."* ~ 1 Corinthians 12:7-11

Basically, a word of knowledge is information (past or present) about a particular person or situation that God is aware of, but we are not. It may come to us as the voice of God speaking or a still small voice. It may come in a dream or vision, and sometimes, just as an impression. The important thing to remember here is when God gives us a piece of information about someone or something, we need to ask Him what He wants us to do with that information. If we don't follow God's will pertaining to a word of knowledge that He gives us, nothing will happen.

Examples of the word of knowledge in the Bible:

- 1 Samuel 9:19-20 → Samuel told Saul the lost donkeys had been found

- 1 Kings 19:18 → Elijah is encouraged by God that he is not the only prophet left

- 2 Kings 6:9-12 → God tells Elisha the enemy's plan

- Luke 19:30-31 → Jesus told His disciples where to find the donkey He was going to ride

- John 4:16-19 → Jesus tells the Samaritan woman at the well that she has no husband

- Acts 9:10-12 → Ananias receives a word about Saul of Tarsus

- Acts 10:9-20 → Peter receives a word about the gospel going to the Gentiles, too

A word of knowledge may be given for many reasons:

- To alert us to a situation that God would like to address

- To encourage or comfort us

- To lead people to Christ

- To let someone know that they CAN be healed

- To encourage US to pray for a condition we might not usually have the faith to pray for

- To reveal sickness

- To give direction

- To restore a believer in fellowship with God and many other reasons

Many people receive words of knowledge every day and don't realize or understand that that is what it is. If you would like to start receiving words of knowledge or be aware that they are coming to you, spend time getting to know Holy Spirit and learn about His ways. Then ask Him to reveal things to you. Be sensitive to His leading and just obey! It really IS that simple. All you have to do is ASK! (James 1:5) Holy Spirit is waiting.

Chapter Fourteen

Glory

"And the glory which You gave Me I have given them, that they may be one just as We are one" ~ John 17:22

The HOPE Center (www.myhopecenter.com) in Belle Vernon, PA, where my parents attend church, was hosting a weekend long "Glory Conference". They had invited a number of different ministries to lead us into deeper levels of glory. There was a ministry that taught flag worship, another did worship art, a Prophet named Randy Chandler was there as the main speaker, and Mike & Cindy Teagarden of Deep Water Ministries International (www.deepwaterhealing.com) were there teaching about miracles and supernatural healing. Each attendee could choose a track to follow and I chose the healing track with the Teagardens. That has been my passion for a long time.

The classes they taught were amazing and simple. Anyone could learn them and use them immediately. I was so excited and stirred up; I could hardly stand it!

During the evening service on Friday, we participated in a Healing and Miracle Service. I was fascinated by everything that was going on around me, especially since I had never experienced a Healing and Miracle Service before! My mom even went up for prayer, so I decided to go and stand behind her with my hand on her shoulder just to show support and to listen to what Cindy was praying about. When Cindy was finished, she moved over in front of me and touched my forehead. I almost stepped away as if to say, "*Oh, I wasn't looking for healing or prayer*", but I stayed because I really wanted to know what she had to say. I was intrigued AND fascinated all at the same time.

Then Cindy said, "*Huh? Hmmmmmm.*"

"*What did THAT mean?*" I wondered.

She stayed there for just a minute, but it felt like FOREVER!

Then she said, "*Wow! I have NEVER seen THAT before!*"

Of course, I said, "*What haven't you seen before?*"

She said, "*I just watched the Lord anoint your feet with oil! What do you think that means?*"

"*I have no idea,*" I replied. What DID that mean? I didn't have the foggiest of ideas, but I sure wanted to know!

Cindy kept praying and next thing I know, I was slain in the Spirit. Down I went! Interestingly enough, I was still cognizant of what was going on around me, but I didn't care about it. Holy Spirit was right there, enveloping me in His light, His peace, and His love.

Then He spoke - ever so quietly, "*Rachel, I have anointed your feet, to remind you that I am right here, walking beside you. Do not walk behind Me, nor do I want you to get ahead of Me - just walk beside me into the anointing and plan I have for your life.*"

That was it. I knew the visitation was over and I opened my eyes to see my mom standing over me. She helped me to my feet and we returned to our seats.

The power of the Holy Spirit is so incredible, so amazing, and yet so gentle. There isn't any fear, there isn't any anger, and there isn't any anxiety. He touches you right in the middle of who you are and you are never the same.

During the healing classes that began the next day, we had the opportunity to practice some of the techniques we were learning on each other. Tonya was my partner and we were practicing "the pelvic thing". I was the recipient and Tonya was praying. As soon as she started, my pelvis started gently turning from side to side. I wasn't doing it and neither was she. The Holy Spirit was ALL UP IN MY BUSINESS! Yes, He most certainly was!

How do I know? Because most of the past ten years had been filled with a mild, but constant low back pain, but ever since I had that Holy Spirit chiropractic adjustment, I have never suffered from low back pain again.

The Holy Spirit is VERY real! He's VERY alive! He cares about even the little things, like low back pain. It is His desire to heal. He is the same, yesterday, today, and forever (Hebrews 13:8). He cannot lie (Titus 1:2) and He loves you and me (John 3:16).

That wonderful weekend was filled with so much of God's glory. We saw gold spots on various walls within the church. Many were healed and set free! Praise and worship was in abundance, and God's glory flowed everywhere! People who had not gone to church for quite some time were once again ignited and on fire for God. New friendships were formed. Relationships were created. People were saved, healed, set free, AND delivered. It was a weekend filled with encounters with the Holy Spirit. Praise and worship does that, you know! The Holy Spirit cannot stay away when there is praise and worship! He loves it!

The last part of that weekend that touched me personally was the Fire Tunnel. What is a fire tunnel you might ask? It's challenging to explain, but I will make a strong effort to do just that. Two lines are formed, parallel to each other, with the leaders of the event. Everyone else forms a single file line and one by one, each person enters the "fire tunnel" - the gifts of the Spirit are released and/or stirred up. Words of wisdom and words of knowledge are spoken over the person. Healings, miracles, and deliverances occur. It's a tunnel where the Holy Spirit is focused and on fire. It's an incredible experience, and although people respond to it differently, EVERYONE is touched by His presence and His fire. That's why it's called a fire tunnel.

Some of the words spoken over me included the activation of the nine gifts of the Holy Spirit. My tongue was "released" to speak with boldness and confidence. I was told that I would be the author of over 30 books - THIS being the first one! Someone else told me that I would be bringing finances into the Kingdom and guiding others to do the same. Another person revealed my compassion for the mentally challenged, including addictions, depression, and oppression. There aren't too many people who are aware of that about me and to have that revealed was very comforting and exciting.

HE CONVICTS. I REPENT. HE FORGIVES.

Has everything that was spoken over me that day happened? Not yet, but I'm not worried. Holy Spirit has my life in control. Do I miss the mark at times? You bet, but He doesn't mind, nor is He surprised. He convicts. I repent. He forgives. It really is that simple!

So, what is this stuff called glory? If you run around in charismatic or Pentecostal circles, you may often hear phrases like "Enter into His glory", or "The glory is descending", or maybe even "experiencing His glory". I don't know about you, but it took me a long time to really understand what that meant. So, this will be my elementary attempt to explain what I have come to discover about "The glory".

I found a pretty good description of the glory in Revelations 15:8, AMP.

> *"And the sanctuary was filled with smoke from the glory (the radiance, the splendor) of God and from His might and power,..."*

THE GLORY IS THE PRESENCE OF GOD. The glory is the Presence of God. It's all He is, His radiance, His splendor, His power, and His might. We all know that when man tries to define the things of God, we usually end up messing things up (just look at the Pharisees). Defining God and/or His glory using mere words is very challenging in my opinion because no one could ever define or describe all that God is. However, I want to give it a good ole college try and see where we end up.

God has been appearing to man throughout the entire Bible. In Genesis 3:8, we learn that Adam and Eve "*heard the sound of the Lord*" and hid themselves from His presence. They knew Him by His presence. He appeared to some people in visions, while He spoke to others without appearing to them. Sometimes He appeared in human form, while other times He appeared as an angel. He didn't always appear the same every time. He wrestled with Jacob (Genesis 32:22-32), appeared in a burning bush to Moses (Exodus 3:1-22), and as a still small voice to Elijah (1 Kings 19:11-12).

Saul (1 Samuel 10:9-13), Balaam (Numbers 23-24), and Zacharias (Luke 1:67) "felt" the Spirit and prophesied during His presence. God has been seen, felt, heard, etc., during earthquakes, storms, darkness, lightning, and thunder. Some have described hearing trumpets or shouting, while others have seen Him as a radiant light. Thousands saw Him as Jesus Christ and 500 were privileged to see the Resurrected Lord before He ascended to the right hand of the Father (1 Corinthians 15:3-11). Peter, James, and John saw Jesus in all His glory on the Mount of Transfiguration (Matthew 17:1-9), and Stephen got to see Him when he (meaning Stephen) was stoned to death (Acts 7:55).

The point I am trying to make here is that we should not limit God's presence, or His glory, to one particular form or manifestation. His glory can and will appear in many different ways, as long as we don't hinder Him by our limited views of Who

He is! Faith can be limited and sometimes destroyed by our inability to allow God to be God. Limiting faith, limits God. We need to spend time meditating on scriptures like 1 Kings 8:27, which says,

> *"... behold, heaven and the heaven of heavens cannot contain you..."*

Our minds can't even begin to understand God and all that He is. Confining Him and His Glory to a box is doing Him (and us) a great disservice, because God is so much more far-reaching and transcendent than that. If we become too familiar with our own conception of God, we start limiting what God can do.

In Exodus chapter 33, Moses is talking with God after the golden calf incident. God is mad and Moses is trying to get His mind wrapped around it all. This is when He asks God to show him His glory.

> **17** *"So the LORD said to Moses, "I will also do this thing that you have spoken; for you have found grace in My sight, and I know you by name." **18** And he said, "Please, show me Your glory." **19** Then He said, "I will make all My goodness pass before you, and I will proclaim the name of the LORD before you. I will be gracious to whom I will be gracious, and I will have compassion on whom I will have compassion." **20** But He said, "You cannot see My face; for no man shall see Me, and live." **21** And the LORD said, "Here is a place by Me, and you shall stand on the rock. **22** So it shall be, while My glory passes by, that I will put you in the cleft of the rock, and will cover you with My hand while I pass by. **23** Then I will take away My hand, and you shall see My back; but My face shall not be seen."*

Did you see how God described His glory?

To God, His Glory is His Holy, righteous, perfect character. It is the essential essence of Who He is. That is what is glorious to God, His goodness, His character—that's what makes Him God. He's holy and righteous and the ultimate definition of goodness! He is the perfection of Love, Grace, and Truth. He is our Provider, our Healer, our Protector, and our Deliverer. He is also our Rear Guard, our King, our Savior, our Strong tower, our Guide, our Counselor, and so much more! The real glory of God is found in His long-suffering, His mercy, His goodness and truth, and His forgiveness as described in Exodus 34:5-7.

> *5 Now the LORD descended in the cloud and stood with him there, and proclaimed the name of the LORD. 6 And the LORD passed before him and proclaimed, "The LORD, the LORD God, merciful and gracious, longsuffering, and abounding in goodness and truth, 7 keeping mercy for thousands, forgiving iniquity and transgression and sin, by no means clearing the guilty, visiting the iniquity of the fathers upon the children and the children's children to the third and the fourth generation."*

Now in John 1:14, we read another description of the glory.

> *"And the Word became flesh and dwelt among us, and we beheld His glory, the glory as of the only begotten of the Father, full of grace and truth."*

Do you see how He defines glory? FULL OF GRACE AND TRUTH. It's EVERYTHING God is! Grace encompassing the beauty of God's love towards us and truth encompassing all of the revelations God has been sharing with us from the beginning. Both parts of His glory can be transferred to us! Let's take a look at John 17:20-22.

> *20 "I do not pray for these alone [the eleven that were with Him], but also for those who will believe in Me through their word [that's us]; 21 that they all may be one, as You, Father, are in Me, and I in You; that they*

> *also may be one in Us, that the world may believe that You sent Me.* **22** *And the glory which You gave Me I have given them... [He transferred it to us]... that they may be one just as We are one:"*

When we receive the glory of God and exhibit it in our lives, we become unified with the Father, Son, and Holy Spirit and share in the same glory that They do! When God is present, His glory is present and therefore, ANYTHING can happen.

So, how does He share His glory with us? He releases it though miracles, signs, and wonders!

- Angelic encounters (1 Kings 19:5-7; Acts 10:3, 12:7-11)

- Flame of fire (Exodus 40:38; Acts 2:3)

- Loud trumpet blast (Exodus 19:9,16)

- Water transformed into wine (John 2:1-11)

- As a cloud (Exodus 40:36; 2 Chronicles 5:13-14)

- Financial miracles (Matthew 17:27)

- Dew upon clothes (Judges 6:37-38)

- A pool of healing water (John 5:1-15)

- A mighty rushing wind (Acts 2:2)

- Manna (aka provision) (Exodus 16)

The glory draws us closer to Him because it declares Who He is - a miraculous God! Think about it. Hebrews 13:8 tells us:

> *"Jesus is the same yesterday, today, and forever."*

If He performed through miracles, signs, and wonders in biblical times, He will continue to do so during our time. That just gets me so excited I can hardly stand it!

It only gets better! WE, as followers of Jesus Christ are carriers of this glory. Don't believe me? Check out 1 Corinthians 3:16.

> *"Don't you know that you yourselves are God's temple and that God's Spirit dwells in your midst?"*

God's Spirit DWELLS within us (1 John 4:4). God's glory - WHO HE IS, lives inside of us. I struggle to even wrap my mind around that concept. The God of the Universe (and everything else) CHOOSES to live inside of me (and you, too)!

Ok, great! The glory lives inside of us, but how do we get it outside of us so we can see a difference in the world around us? Well, let's take a look at Psalm 100:4 and see what the Word of God has to say.

> *"Enter into His gates with thanksgiving, And into His courts with praise."*

We open the gates of heaven with thanksgiving and then receive permission to enter His court with our praise. Why do we want to enter His court? Because that's where the glory is! Now that we know how to gain access to the glory, we need to learn how to open the heavens and bring His glory to earth. In Habakkuk 2:14, it is prophesied that the earth will be covered with the knowledge of the glory.

> *"For the earth will be filled with the knowledge of the glory of the LORD, as the waters cover the sea."*

This means that when we begin to understand the glory, how it works, what it feels like, how we can manifest it in our homes, at our jobs, in our churches, we will truly be carriers of His glory. As each of us begin to understand and manifest the glory, we will become carriers of His glory cloud and play a part in Habakkuk's prophecy, helping it to become part of our reality. As we begin to spend time in worship, praising and thanking Him, the heavens WILL open and the glory WILL manifest.

Now, there are a few steps we should be taking to bring the glory into our homes and/or our lives.

1. Wash in the blood of Jesus.

   - Remember, John the Baptist said, "*Repent! for the kingdom of heaven is near!*" (Matthew 3:1-2)

   - Remember, JESUS said, "*Repent! for the kingdom of heaven is at hand!*" (Matthew 4:17)

   - The blood removes any hindrances in us that might cause the heavens to remain closed. When we repent and are washed in the blood, the heavens will open.

   - Matthew 5:20 tells us that we need to be even more righteous than the Pharisees to enter the kingdom of heaven. That's only possible by repentance and washing in the blood. Our righteousness is in Christ Jesus! HE is our righteousness!

   - Ephesians 1:7-9 explains to us that we have redemption through the blood of Jesus. He pours out His wisdom and understanding, and makes the secret of His will (which is to unify all things in heaven AND earth) known to us. These scriptures show us how heaven and earth come together at the cross.

   - When we are washed in the blood, it removes ALL hindrances, opening the gates of heaven and allowing the glory to fall down.

2. Spend focused time in thanksgiving and prayer.

- We offer a sacrifice of praise. How do we do that? We contend to keep our focus and in doing so, we honor God by keeping our minds fixed on Him. This is when the breakthrough that we are looking for comes-- when we keep our mind FIXED on Him while we are praising and thanking Him. Here's one important fact. YOU WILL BE DISTRACTED. The devil and his army are very good at that. It's going to happen; it happens to EVERYONE. However, when you take your mind away from those distracting thoughts and re-focus on Jesus, you are showing Him how much you love Him.

3. What to do if you get stuck:

- Think about what's distracting you and release it to God.

- Use your prayer language, also known as praying in the Holy Ghost or the Spirit. It clears out distractions, helps you to focus, and chases away the demons who are whispering in your ear.

- Hebrews 4:11 tells us to *labor into His rest*. Keep re-focusing. God honors what you are doing. He will step in to help you by releasing a spirit of worship. So, don't give up or get discouraged. This spirit of worship prevents the demons from talking with you. They can't stand it and promptly leave. You will recognize this when it happens because your mind will get quiet and it won't be so challenging to focus on Him.

This leads me nicely into the last thing I wanted to mention about the glory. How do we know when the glory comes?

1. Faith. Ask Jesus if it is present. He will usually answer you with a scripture.

2. The atmosphere changes. Your mind is quiet and peaceful.

3. Feels like a sunburn. When the glory landed on Jesus at the Mount of Transfiguration, it appeared as a bright light.

4. You may feel a heaviness, like something is pushing on your head, neck, and/or shoulders. In Hebrew, the glory is called the Kobad. The root of the word Kobad is defined as heavy or weighty.

These are just some of the ways you might recognize the glory. Trust me, there are many more! Don't limit God's glory by trying to predict how it's going to manifest. Just allow it to manifest in any way God chooses.

Once the glory manifests, choose to pursue it every day, wherever you are. Stop praying, meditating, or studying the Word without the glory! As you learn, learn about the glory and begin manifesting it into your environment. You will find God working all types of breakthroughs and miracles in your life and the lives of those in your world!

Chapter Fifteen

Crisis Response

"Bear one another's burdens, and so fulfill the law of Christ."
~ Galatians 6:2

I attended a weeklong training seminar hosted by an organization called, Crisis Response International (www.criout.com). Their mission is to reach the lost in crisis. They send resources and trained volunteers to assist the relief effort at disasters all around the world. One of the many desires of my heart is to help people when they need it the most. I have dreamed of being on a rapid response team for most of my adult life. Probably one of the many reasons I became a paramedic and then an emergency nurse.

At this seminar, they taught us many things like how to minister in crisis, spiritual and emotional care, Critical Incident Stress Management, first-aid, pre-hospital care, water purification, sanitation, food security, personal and community preparedness, the four phases of disaster, disaster operations and protocol, building cities of refuge, scene safety and assessment, and many other things. What makes this organization so unique is how involved the Holy Spirit is. I believe the reason for this is how much worship we were involved in every day!

There were 150 of us at this particular camp, divided into five separate teams. You stayed with your team of thirty for all of the training and practical sessions. We worshipped with our team in the morning before breakfast and then with the camp after breakfast before our group trainings. The afternoons were spent training. After dinner, we worshipped some more before our evening classes. It was an amazing time of learning and growing, and fellowship with others and the Lord. I loved every minute!

****

One of the highlights for me happened on the second day of training. The day started as every other day with breakfast, followed by an amazing time of camp worship before we started our classes. This particular morning, my heart was very heavy as I was crying out to the Lord. I remember, as if it was yesterday, the intense longing I had to just worship at His feet, but I didn't know how. The pain in my heart was intense! Tears abundantly flowed down my cheeks as I cried silently, wanting to experience Him the way it "appeared" everyone else was.

Halfway through this sacred time, Lisa, one of my teammates (and cabin mates), laid her hands on my shoulders. She left them there for quite some time and when the time of worship had ended, she just enveloped me in a hug and told me the Lord had given her a word for me. During our next break, we met over in the corner of the room and this is what she shared.

"*While I was praying for you, the Lord told me that He wanted to speak into your identity and your destiny. When I asked Him about your destiny, He showed me how He had imparted a "Braveheart" courage into you... something that makes you excited about adventure. He also wanted to highlight the name "Beautiful Warrior", with emphasis on the "Beautiful". I could feel His delight in you and how He loved to just gaze on your beauty. He's so proud of the lovely masterpiece He created when He made you..... Even when you don't feel beautiful, He calls you dark, yet lovely. The destiny part came to me in a picture of a "hope chest". It's like there were items in this chest that had been added through the years. I could see that the Lord was encouraging you to take them out and bring them before Him. He wanted you to be reassured that you had not 'heard wrong' but just needed to trust Him with how and when things will come to pass. He also wanted you to not fret or worry that "it's too late" for these promises. He is still actively engaged in preparing the stage for it all."*

As I wrote in an earlier chapter, it's important to evaluate what others claim to be hearing from God. You have to place it against scripture and compare it to what God has already been showing you. This specific word, to me, was a direct answer to the prayers that were coming straight from my heart at that very moment! You have no idea how loved by God I felt after hearing the answer to the cry of my heart.

Let me ask you a question. Have you ever prayed for someone else? I don't mean, "*Hey, Lord, could you please help Mike with whatever he's going through right now?*" I'm talking about a prayer like, "*Lord, please use me today to help someone encounter You.*" Perhaps you were the one praying for God to bring someone like that into your life, someone who was willing to be the answer to YOUR prayer.

Holy Spirit can use any person or situation to answer the prayers of His children. How many times have you received answers to a prayer from someone who wasn't even aware that THEY were the answer to your prayer? I bet it's happened more times than you realize. Now think about this: "What if we were intentional about it?" What I mean by that is, what if we asked Holy Spirit to use us to answer the prayers of His children and then went about searching out those opportunities?

HOLY SPIRIT CAN USE ANY PERSON OR SITUATION TO ANSWER THE PRAYERS OF HIS CHILDREN.

Don't you think we just might be able to change the world? I think that's exactly what would happen. Holy Spirit changing the world through His children, what a concept!

Do you think giving the man standing on the corner a few bucks will make a difference in his life? Maybe, maybe not, but what if it did? What about that mom who just needs a few hours break from her children to refresh and return a better mom? What about the elderly neighbor down the street who might need their toilet fixed, but due to their limited funds have not been able get it done? What if you just allowed Holy Spirit to show you the young woman struggling to connect with God because she just doesn't feel worthy enough to be in His presence?

Jesus told us in Matthew, chapter 25, verses 34-36:

> **34** *Then the King will say to those on His right hand, 'Come, you blessed of My Father, inherit the kingdom prepared for you from the foundation of the world:* **35** *for I was hungry and you gave Me food; I was thirsty and you gave Me drink; I was a stranger and you took Me in;* **36** *I was naked and you clothed Me; I was sick and you visited Me; I was in prison and you came to Me.'*

What if we, as Believers, ACTUALLY did those things? What if...

- We went out of our way to help others?

- We sacrificed our comforts or conveniences to help others?

- We sacrificed our time, our money, or even our safety to help others?

- We befriended the homeless person and helped them to find a job?

Jesus was the ultimate answer to prayer! He sacrificed:

- His comforts of home by traveling to share an unpopular message

[121]

- His body when He allowed Himself to be flogged and beaten
- His pride when He chose not to defend Himself

- His life when He voluntarily died so that we might live

Jesus gave everything He had for each one of us. EVERYTHING! We, as Believers, followers of the Lord Jesus Christ, should be more than willing to sacrifice EVERYTHING for Him...

Paul sacrificed his comfort and safety to reach the Gentiles. Peter, James, and John sacrificed their comfort and safety to reach the Jews. Mother Theresa sacrificed her comfort and safety to comfort the poor. My friends Ben and Michelle sacrifice their comfort and safety, today, serving the unreached people groups of Narnia. Many have lost their lives in service to those who have never even heard of Jesus, let alone met Him.

If we challenge ourselves to do more and to be more available to be used by the Holy Spirit, I believe we will have greater results. Let's be real here, Holy Spirit doesn't NEED us for anything. He is quite capable of bringing His plans into fruition without us, but I believe that it brings Him great joy to partner with us in bringing change into the lives of the people He has put around us. Stepping out in faith with Him will be scary, uncomfortable, and maybe even risky, but it will be so worth it and it might just change the world.

Holy Spirit is the one who answers prayer, but how wonderful will it be to be the tool He uses to bring about the change He wants to see in the world?

Chapter Sixteen

The Cross at Jumonville

"I ask-ask the God of our Master, Jesus Christ, the God of glory - to make you intelligent and discerning in knowing him personally, your eyes focused and clear, so that you can see exactly what it is he is calling you to do, grasp the immensity of this glorious way of life he has for his followers, oh, the utter extravagance of his work in us who trust him-endless energy, boundless strength!" ~ Ephesians 1:17-19 MSG

In January of 2011, I began a new ministry with my parents through the H.O.P.E. (House of Prayer and Evangelism) Center; in Belle Vernon, Pennsylvania called Rivers of Healing Ministries, (You can check us out at http://www.riversofhealing.com/). Our main purpose is to teach the body of Christ that God still heals through His children today. AND, He CAN and WILL do it through us!

After a year of teaching and ministry, we wanted to hold a retreat that would bless and encourage our team. Our mentors, Mike and Cindy Teagarden and their Deep Water Ministries team were invited to participate as well. We were looking for a great place where we could get away from the trials of our lives for a few days and bask in the Presence of God while we refreshed and fellowshipped with each other. Father God provided Jumonville.

Jumonville is a premier Christian Camp and Retreat Center located about 50 miles south of Pittsburgh in the beautiful mountains of South Western Pennsylvania. Since 1950, a steel cross has stood sixty feet high on a six-foot tall concrete base on

Dunbar's Knob, which is 2,480 feet above sea level. On a clear day, the mountaintop boasts a view of three states and seven counties with sights up to 50 miles away. At night, it is bathed in glowing spotlights, shining as a beacon of hope and inspiration to all who see it far above the dark silhouette of the Appalachian Mountains.

Saturday afternoon, a group of us decided to hike up to the cross. It was a little more intense of a walk than we expected, but everyone made it to the top. We walked around enjoying the view and the beauty of this amazing cross and then gathered in a circle, holding hands, and began praying in the Spirit. Prophecies were spoken and words of our hearts and His were spoken. We worshipped and praised our Lord and Savior for what He had done for us on the cross and through His resurrection. It was an amazing time in the Presence of the Lord.

During this time, Jesus showed me a wonderful picture. It began with Him, in the center of our circle. He had tears in His eyes as He walked around the circle, touching each one of our faces and kissing us on the cheek. He spoke words of love and encouragement over each one of us, and He shared how proud He was of all the things we were accomplishing for His glory. Then, I saw fire flying out of each one of us, straight up into the sky until, at about ten feet above us, all the individual flames converged into one flame that continued shooting up into the heavens and I heard the word, "Unity".

I believe this second part of the picture was Jesus showing me how powerful our individual flames were and how much that power was magnified when we were all united in spirit, soul, and body towards His purposes. What an exciting time to be alive!

Holy Spirit sometimes speaks to us in pictures. Have you EVER received a picture, a vision, or dream from God? Well, He uses our imagination to imprint pictures in our minds that exhort, edify, encourage, empower, and uplift. It's not a picture that you can see with your natural eyes, but with your spiritual eyes (see

Ephesians 1:17-19). This picture, seen with your spiritual eyes, is actually MORE real than ANY picture you would see with your physical eyes AND has the power behind it to bring change into your life. It takes faith to see these pictures, to learn from these pictures, and to change from these pictures.

How do we see these pictures?

> Psalm 119:18 says, "*Open my eyes, that I may see Wondrous things from Your law.*"

To me, this one small scripture is saying a whole lot! It's obviously not talking about our natural vision because we can open our natural eyes ourselves. So, we must have another set of eyes to "see" things with. I would like to say the author of this verse is referring to our spiritual eyes. When I experienced those pictures described above, it was with my spiritual eyes that I was seeing those things.

In Ephesians 1:17-19, Paul prays that God will enlighten the eyes of our hearts.

> "*I ask—ask the God of our Master, Jesus Christ, the God of glory—to make you intelligent and discerning in knowing him personally, your eyes focused and clear, so that you can see exactly what it is he is calling you to do, grasp the immensity of this glorious way of life he has for his followers, oh, the utter extravagance of his work in us who trust him—endless energy, boundless strength!*" MSG

THE EYES IN OUR HEADS SEE THE TRUTH, AND THE EYES OF OUR HEARTS FEEL THE TRUTH.

This means we have two sets of eyes — eyes in our heads and eyes in our hearts. The eyes in our heads SEE the truth, and the eyes of our hearts FEEL the truth.

Why is there a difference?

[125]

Well, sin is like a cataract growing over the eyes of our heart (2 Corinthians 4:4). When we learn that it is ok to trust Jesus, He cuts away those cataracts, which allows us to see into the spirit realm more clearly. We not only "see" the truth He is revealing to our natural eyes, but we also "feel" that truth in our hearts. The problem comes because of the sin that is still present within us. It's like the mold that won't die. If it's not removed from within, it will continue to re-grow and block us from experiencing truth as we were created to experience it.

The beauty of the gospel and our amazing relationship with the Holy Spirit is we have access to the Holy Spirit 24 hours a day, seven days a week. We just have to ask Him to open the eyes of our hearts and He will! I learned that if I am struggling to see with my spiritual eyes or see into the spirit realm; that is when the cataracts of sin are blinding me. Thankfully, the Holy Spirit is a perfectly skilled eye-surgeon who specializes in cutting away these cataracts. So, if you are struggling with your spiritual eyesight, don't give up! Don't be discouraged! Instead, call on Holy Spirit. He is just waiting to surgically repair your eyes!

THE BEAUTY OF THE GOSPEL AND OUR AMAZING RELATIONSHIP WITH THE HOLY SPIRIT IS WE HAVE ACCESS TO THE HOLY SPIRIT 24 HOURS A DAY, SEVEN DAYS A WEEK.

Seeing with spiritual eyes encompasses a number of different things.

1. Engaging in the hope of your calling (Ephesians 1:18)

2. Centering your life on Jesus (Hebrews 12:2)

3. Recognizing the presence of Holy Spirit (Luke 24:31)

4. Discovering revelation in the Word of God (Psalm 119:18)

5. Pinpointing opportunities for evangelism (John 4:35)

6. Discerning the spiritual realm (2 Kings 6:17)

There are three keys to enhancing your ability to use your "spiritual eyes".

1. **Spending time in the presence of God**

The more time we spend in the presence of God, the more He will enable us to see. Here's how it works. There is light wherever God is. Darkness can't stand the Light. In the natural, we need light to be able to see. Well, the same thing applies in the spiritual realm. If you are living in darkness, you won't be able to see anything, but as you spend time in His presence, the darkness flees and it becomes easier and easier to see.

Let's take a look at a few supportive scriptures.

> *"This is the message which we have heard from Him and declare to you, that God is light and in Him is no darkness at all."* ~ 1 John 1:5

> *"I have come as a light into the world, that whoever believes in Me should not abide in darkness."* ~ John 12:46

> *"He has delivered us from the power of darkness and conveyed us into the kingdom of the Son of His love."* ~ Colossians 1:13

> *"But you are a chosen generation, a royal priesthood, a holy nation, His own special people, that you may proclaim the praises of Him who called you out of darkness into His marvelous light."* ~ 2 Peter 1:9

> "But if we walk in the light as He is in the light, we have fellowship with one another, and the blood of Jesus Christ His Son cleanses us from all sin." ~ 1 John 1:7

2. **Exercise your spiritual eyes**

When it comes to spiritual eyes, usually the problem is not that they are closed, but rather that they are blinded.

> 2 Corinthians 4:4 says, *"The god of this age [satan] has blinded the minds of unbelievers, so that they cannot see the light of the gospel that displays the glory of Christ, who is the image of God."*

In the natural realm, blindness isn't fixed by merely opening one's eyes. Well, the same goes for the spiritual realm. The only solution is healing, and the only source for that healing is Jesus Christ.

> Isaiah 42:7 – *[God the Father sent Jesus] to open eyes that are blind, to free captives from prison and to release from the dungeon those who sit in darkness.*

> Revelation 3:15-19 – ***15** [Jesus said,] "I know your deeds, that you are neither cold nor hot. I wish you were either one or the other! **16** So, because you are lukewarm–neither hot nor cold–I am about to spit you out of my mouth. **17** You say, 'I am rich; I have acquired wealth and do not need a thing.'* **But you do not realize that you are wretched, pitiful, poor, blind and naked. 18** *I counsel you to buy from me gold refined in the fire so you can become rich; and white clothes to wear, so you can cover your shameful nakedness;* **and salve to put on your eyes, so you can see.** *19 Those whom I love I rebuke and discipline. So be earnest and repent."* (emphasis added)

We cannot open our own spiritual eyes. All we can do is come to

Christ the Healer and humbly cry out for Him to awaken them. Repentance is a gift from God (Acts 5:31), so we can't successfully do it in our own strength.

Only Jesus can open your spiritual eyes, so make Him the center of your life in all things. Whenever it seems that you can't see spiritually, talk to Him about it. He wants to open your eyes.

3. **Exercise Your Spiritual Senses**

We all know that after an injury or a major illness, we need to take time to exercise and/or strengthen our bodies. When it comes to our physical eyes, the more we use them, the more we are able to do with them. By reason of use, we learn to read, distinguish faces, sense danger, and recognize familiar places.

Remember when you were learning to drive? How you had to use your eyes to rapidly take in everything they could while speeding by? Before you learned how to drive, you could only process your surroundings at a rate as fast as you could run, but while driving, you have to process information much more quickly. Sometimes, as fast as 70-75 miles per hour. You train your physical eyes to drive safely and effectively. It's no different with your spiritual senses. By using your spiritual eyes regularly, your discernment is strengthened (Hebrews 5:14).

When Jesus opened the Apostle Paul's spiritual eyes, He gave him a mission.

> *"I will deliver you from the Jewish people, as well as from the Gentiles, to whom I now send you, to open their eyes, in order to turn them from darkness to light, and from the power of satan to God, that they may receive forgiveness of sins and an inheritance among those who are sanctified by faith in Me."* ~ Acts 26:17-18

If we are walking in the light, then we need to show others how wonderful it is in the Light; How wonderful Father God, His Son

Jesus, and the Holy Spirit are! Testify of the hope that we have found in Jesus. Show them:

- How to see into the spiritual realm

- How to discover revelation in the Word of God

- How to recognize the presence of Jesus everyday

- How to share their testimony with others

- How to keep their life focused on Jesus Christ

Are your spiritual eyes open? Have you encountered the Light? Are you sharing it with others?

Chapter Seventeen

The Fragrance of God

"For we are the sweet fragrance of Christ unto God among those who are being saved and among those perishing:" ~ 2 Corinthians 2:15

In March of 2010, I received the phone call that I had been dreading for some time. My maternal grandfather, Robert Meek (aka Pap Pap), had taken a turn for the worse with his health and had less than a week to live. He had been battling Congestive Heart Failure (aka CHF) for a few years and his heart was just about done. So, I did what anyone else would do in this situation. I rearranged my schedule and headed home to speak to my Pap just one more time before he headed off into the arms of Jesus.

I come from a large family. Mom has four brothers and two sisters. There are seventeen grandchildren, six to eight great grandchildren, plus spouses, girl/boyfriends, etc. So, his last weekend was pretty busy as everyone went to Pennsylvania to say good-bye. I believe my fifteen to twenty minutes with him were the best. My Pap was sitting in his chair and he asked me if I had EVER smelled the fragrance of God. At first, I thought maybe he was confused or something, but after a moment or two, I realized that he wasn't. He told me that God has many different scents and they are very difficult to describe. Pap told me that he ALWAYS knew when God's presence was near because he could smell Him and, that His fragrance had been around a lot this past week and it was stronger than he had ever smelled before.

[131]

He also told me that he had been seeing a lot of new colors that he had never seen before. Again, he asked me if I had ever gotten a glimpse of colors I had never seen before. I told him that I had not. We both just sat there for a few minutes with our eyes closed, knowing this was probably the last time we would have together until I joined him in heaven with Jesus.

He opened his eyes a moment or so later, reached out his hands, and placed them on my head.

Then he said to me, "*Rachel, Holy Spirit has directed me to impart those gifts to you.*"

"*What gifts are those, Pap?*" I asked.

"*The ability to smell the fragrance of God and to see into the spirit realm,*" he said.

Humbly, I bowed my head and shed a few tears as my grandfather imparted those gifts to me, knowing that was probably the last thing I would ever receive from him. I didn't really understand what he was giving to me at the time, but I knew that I wanted whatever he had to give. I knew that it would make a difference in my life someday.

A year or so later, my family hosted our good friends from Deep Water Ministries (DWM) for a weekend of teaching, learning, fellowship, healing, AND deliverance. Classes were held at the H.O.P.E. Center in Monongahela, Pennsylvania and the team stayed with us at my parent's home. It was an incredible weekend! We were so blessed by everything that happened.

During the Sunday service, we had an amazing time of worship, followed by miracles, signs, and wonders. It was a fantastic time in the presence of the Lord! In fact, I don't recall a time when the presence was stronger than what we felt that morning. After the service was over, we headed back to my parents' house with the team from Deep Water Ministries to share one final meal together before they headed back to Ohio.

Just as we were sitting down to dinner, one of DWM team members realized that she had left her jacket at the church. Ugh! Really? I knew I was going to have to go back to the church to get it and I did NOT want to go. Thankfully, my parents raised me better than that, so I grabbed my keys to head back to the church (which, by the way, was only 10 minutes away). My poor attitude and I asked my friend Charlotte if she minded riding back to the church to get this jacket. She knew how I was feeling, so she readily agreed to make the trip with me. Thank you, Charlotte!

We jumped into my Jeep and off we went. As we opened the doors of the church, we were both hit with the most amazing smell. At first, I didn't say anything. I figured it was the flowers left in the sanctuary or maybe the remnants of someone's perfume. However, as we walked closer and closer to the altar, the fragrance got stronger and stronger. I KNEW that I had NEVER smelled that fragrance before. Most strong scents make me really nauseated, but the stronger this scent became, the more pleasing it became. I turned to Charlotte and asked her, "*Do you smell that?*"

She immediately responded, "*Yeah. I was going to ask you if you knew what it was.*"

Right then, never having had a thought like that before in my life, I knew Holy Spirit was revealing to me that it was the fragrance of God. It was one of those times where, you know, that you Know, that you KNOW, you are hearing from God. When I told Charlotte that it was the fragrance of God, she told me that it had witnessed with her, that it was in fact, the fragrance of God. The closer we got to the altar, the stronger it became.

Now, a more mature disciple would have dropped to their knees, lain prostrate on the ground for as long as that fragrance was present, and just worshipped God. Ha! Not me! I grabbed that jacket, ran to my Jeep, and hurried back to share what had just happened to us with everyone at my parents' house. Everyone was so excited to hear about what we had just experienced! Many people told us that God had witnessed to them that we had indeed experienced the fragrance of God.

What an honor and a privilege that was! I wish I had understood it better at the time. However, what really stood out to me from that experience was the fact that Holy Spirit chose to share it with me, in spite of my poor attitude. He gave me one of the most incredible gifts - His fragrance - an aroma that I can't describe or define; an aroma that was more pleasing than any other smell that I have ever experienced; and one that I will NEVER forget!

Now I want to ask you a question. Have you ever been in a room with someone who was wearing an amazing perfume or cologne? Of course, you have. We have all had that experience at least once in our lives. What about the fragrance that your husband, wife, boyfriend, or girlfriend wears all the time? Don't you know they have entered the room by the scent they are wearing?

In the book of Esther, we learn how Esther spent an entire year being prepared to become the wife of the King. Every day for that entire year, she was anointed with scented oils in preparation for her first meeting with the king. Scripture tells us that the king was captivated by her fragrance of grace and beauty. The point I am trying to make is that there was a period of preparation before she was exalted. Because of her willingness to submit to the process of preparation, she eventually became royalty and saved the lives of the entire nation of Israel.

Have you ever wondered what God smells like? Have you ever really thought about it? In 2 Corinthians 2:15, the Apostle Paul tells us that as disciples of Christ, we exude the fragrance of Christ:

"*For we are to God the fragrance of Christ*"

What that means, basically, is that from spending time with Christ, worshiping Him, His presence rubs off onto us and we begin to emanate His scent. Did you read that? A scent, an aroma, a fragrance MUST emanate from Him, for us to smell like Him. In Hebrews 1:8-9 we read,

> **8**"*But to the Son He says: 'Your throne, O God, is forever and ever; A scepter of righteousness is the scepter of Your kingdom.* **9** *You have loved righteousness and hated lawlessness; Therefore God,* **our God, has anointed You with the oil of gladness** *more than Your companions.*"

The more time we spend with our Lord and Savior, the more we are going to be covered in His anointing oil, and the more we are going to emanate His amazing anointed royal fragrance.

> "*We are a chosen generation, a royal priesthood, a holy nation, a peculiar people, who will show forth the praise of Him, Who has called us out of darkness, into His marvelous light.*" ~ 1 Peter 2:9

We all know that perfumes are made from many different ingredients. Different combinations of various ingredients create many different scents or fragrances. Such is true of the fragrance of God. In the book of Galatians, Paul lists all of the characteristics that make up God's true nature. These characteristics of God are the ingredients that form His unique fragrance.

> "*The fruit of the Spirit is love, joy, peace, patience, kindness, goodness, faithfulness, gentleness and self-control. Against such things there is no law.*" ~ Galatians 5:22-23.

Spending time in His presence creates these amazing characteristics within us and when the right amounts of each fruit are evidenced in our lives, we will indeed exude the amazing fragrance that can only come from God. True worship produces the precise ingredients of God's nature in us. As we continue to return to His presence in worship, we are infused over and over again with His nature, His characteristics, and His fragrance.

In Luke 4:16-21, Jesus tells us that He was the fulfillment of Isaiah 61:1-3.

> *"The Spirit of the Lord is upon me..."*

Everyone wanted to be near Jesus because the fragrance of the Holy Spirit emanated from Him. It was intoxicating. It changed people's lives. Jesus was anointed with the oil of joy (See Hebrews 1:9). How did He become anointed with this oil of joy? By spending time in the presence of the Father. How do we know that He did that? Because in John 5:19, He tells us that He did only what He saw the Father do and He didn't do anything that He didn't see the Father do. For Him to know what the Father did, He would have had to spend time with Him.

As we worship, the Father begins to inhabit our worship and we are forever changed. How are we changed? We become one with Him. Can you imagine staying the same after experiencing any member of the Godhead?

As we worship, we grow into His likeness ~ Ephesians 4:13, AMP.

...THE MORE MATURE WE BECOME BY SPENDING TIME WITH HIM, THE STRONGER HIS FRAGRANCE WILL OVERFLOW FROM US.

Worship that brings the fragrance of God into our midst doesn't just come from singing alone. I believe it comes from a life completely submitted to the Holy Spirit, a mind that is continually being renewed by meditating on the Word of God, and a prayer life that matches no other. The Bride of Christ, who is preparing herself to rule and reign with Christ, will become more evident to everyone around her as she matures and begins to emanate that fragrance of Christ. Think about it - the more mature fruit or flowers become, the stronger their fragrance. That can only mean the same thing for those of us preparing to be the bride of Christ - the more mature we become by spending time with Him, the stronger His fragrance will overflow from us.

True worshipers are rising up all over the world. The world WILL start to notice His amazing fragrance emanating from the mature bride of Christ and THEIR lives will never be the same!

Chapter Eighteen

Haiti

"And Jesus came and spoke to them, saying, 'All authority has been given to Me in heaven and on earth. Go therefore and make disciples of all the nations, baptizing them in the name of the Father and of the Son and of the Holy Spirit, teaching them to observe all things that I have commanded you; and lo, I am with you always, even to the end of the age. Amen.'"
~ Matthew 28:18-20

There is no way I could talk about encountering the Holy Spirit without talking about my first trip to Haiti with Joan Hunter Ministries (www.joanhunter.org). Father God has put a HUGE desire in my heart to work with Him all over the world and I was so excited to have this opportunity to go to Haiti.

He planted the seed for me to travel with this ministry back in the fall of 2011. However, when I looked at their requirements to go, I was missing a few and would not be able to complete them prior to their trip in 2012. So, I decided that I would work to be eligible to go in 2013. In September of 2012, I applied to go, but never heard back. Months passed by and nothing. Strangely enough, I was okay with it. I wanted to go, but I just figured it wasn't my time and everything would happen when it was supposed to.

Then on January 15, 2013, I received an email asking if I was still interested in going. Somehow my application/paperwork had been misplaced and now, that they had found it, they had a spot for me on the team. Yes! I was so excited... until... I read further in the email. I needed $500 by the end of the month. My heart sank for just a moment or two. How in the world was I going to come up with $500 in TWO WEEKS? It just seemed like a LOT of money!

So, I prayed about it. God didn't really say much to me at that point, but I had so much peace. I just knew He was going to work it out. I talked about it with my friend, Rae, and she encouraged me to ask my family and friends. *"Surely, you know enough people to help you to go,"* she said. *"Put it out there. What's the worst that can happen? No one chooses to participate and you don't go. That's no different than right now."* She was right. I at least had to try.

So, I started talking about it with a few friends from church. I told my mentor and friend, Ann, what I wanted to do and she reminded me, *"If God wants you to do this, then He has to pay for it!"* She prayed with me and I just KNEW that I was going to Haiti! During worship, Holy Spirit and I talked about it some more and I reminded Him that I needed $2500 to go and He responded, *"Well, I'm planning on giving you $3200 to go."*

I foolishly replied, *"But, I only need $2500..."*

To which He replied, *"But, I'm God!"*

What else could I say?

I wrote my support letter. My friend Rae edited it for me and then I posted it online. I invited all of my friends and family to read the letter. It was a great way to allow people who aren't in my life every day to support me if they chose to, and guess what, they did! Many family and friends participated, including some from my home church, my parent's church, and the ministry I co-lead with my parents (Rivers of Healing Ministries). There were family members, friends that I'm close to, and even friends from high school whom I haven't seen in 25+ years who all participated to help make it happen. When it was all said and done, Holy Spirit brought in $3200 for the trip! He honored His Word (Isaiah 55:8-11) and He honored His daughter. That was an encounter that definitely changed my life and has set me on a path to living out of His provision! (Philippians 4:19)

Holy Spirit was teaching me about provision and how He wants to be my provider. Even after He stepped up in a real way, I still didn't get it. So, He brought my new friends into the equation.

A bunch of women on the team were hanging out and getting to know each other, when I stupidly said something about not being able to afford my house if I wanted to go into full-time ministry.

Well, Courtney about convulsed right out the bed! It's true! She jumped up off that bed so fast and basically said, "*Come on girls, we need to PRAY for our sister, Rachel, right now!*" She started speaking and preaching about finances, prosperity, and provision, and sharing her story how she made God her provider → NOT her J.O.B. Everyone came together in the room and began sharing their stories and how I was there in Haiti to have that poverty mindset removed, once and for all!

The funny thing is, I "knew" what they were saying. I had heard it all before. Joan has been teaching about it for years, but I had never had an encounter with the Holy Spirit like that to make it a permanent part of who I was. THAT was all about to change.

Everyone gathered around me, placing their hands on me, so they could impart what they had to me. Courtney began speaking.

Father, we just thank You, Lord God, for Rachel. We thank You for the anointing and calling that You have on her life, Lord God. Not only do we thank You for that calling and anointing, Lord, but we thank You that You are making it clear to her. Father it seems like she is having some confusion whether or not she should do this or should do that. God, you've given her a vision. You know her calling. You said You know the plans you have for us, to prosper us, to give us an expected end. So, Father, in the name of Jesus, we ask You that in the next few days, even today God, to make it clear to her that that is what you would have her to do.

Father, we silence the enemy. We know that you multiply and NEVER divide. So, Father, we thank You in the name of Jesus that everything that the enemy is trying to bring against her mind is silenced. Now! In the name of Jesus. We thank You that she is going to walk in increased finances, that she is going to walk in prosperity, God. You are beginning to show her Your purpose and Your plan for her life. Thank You, Jesus. We bind the spirit of fear, the spirit of intimidation, Father. We speak boldness. You are the God of no impossibilities. Show her that You're the God of impossibilities. Taste and see that the Lord is good. You are good, God. We thank You for showing her YOUR mercy, YOUR grace. We thank You God for blowing her mind. She IS going to see YOUR hand in her life. Let her know that you have not forgotten her, that you will NEVER forget her, that she is YOUR daughter! She is your favorite! She is the apple of Your eye and it gives You great pleasure, it gives You great pleasure that she is walking in everything that she desires. Give her the desires of her heart. God, she wants her mortgage paid off. God, help her not to try to rationalize this whole thing.

Remove Rachel from Rachel, God. Wherever Rachel is, God, replace her with You. Rachel doesn't have the mental capacity to be able to comprehend Your thoughts and plans that You have for her. So, remove her. We want her gone. Replace her with You, God.

We thank You, Lord God, that the financial miracle and financial breakthrough that You are giving her, God, is going to be a blessing to so many. Thank You, Jesus!

Leslie then said, "*Unshackle her. The Lord says that there are shackles on her feet. Take them off!*"

[141]

Courtney followed with, "*Every spirit that is not like You, God, the bondage of poverty mindset, is now gone in Jesus' name!*"

Leslie again said, "*In Jesus name, those shackles come off NOW! In Jesus' name!*"

Courtney then said, "*You are a foul, you are a tormenting spirit. You must go now! Spirit of worry, you must go now in Jesus' name! Give her peace, God, peace that surpasses all understanding. Let it blow her mind where all the peace and joy are coming from. Show her how to praise and worship You in the midst of everything that is going on. We thank You for the testimony that she is going to share with us, soon! Blow her mind, God! In Jesus' name, Amen!*"

April also had something to say! "*I just break off all the word curses that have been spoken over you - like, "You're not ALL that. And I declare that YOU ARE ALL THAT! And you deserve and WILL receive ALL THAT! In Jesus' name, Amen!*"

Leslie followed with, "*We proclaim freedom over you in Jesus' name!*"

Courtney finished with "*YOU ARE FREE!*"

Others spoke during this precious time, but I could not make out what they were saying on the recording.

How are prayers from others an encounter with Holy Spirit? I can't tell you what happened in the natural except I DID feel something lift off me. How do I know? I felt light and free and like I could take on the world! Even April, one of my teammates, noticed it a few hours later as we were leaving for our final night of the crusade. She told me there was a "lightness" about me and that I was glowing!

Keep reading and you will see how my life changed dramatically while we were ministering on our last night of the crusade. You see, when you have a real encounter with the Holy Spirit, you are changed. You will never be the same. This prayer can be said over anyone else and they can experience the very same freedom I did. How do I know that? Because God does not change (Malachi 3:6; Hebrews 13:8), nor is He a respecter of persons (Acts 10:34). What He does for one person, He WILL do for another. If you don't believe me, try it! Listen to someone who has a testimony of something you are looking for and apply your faith in God, and just wait and see what He will do for you!

****

Earlier that week, Joan Hunter Ministries hosted a two day pastor's conference where we could minister to the local pastors, provide Bibles in their language, spiritual teachings and guidance, LOTS of worship and healings, miracles, signs, and wonders! What a privilege to serve such humble servants WITH humble servants! Holy Spirit was so strong during those meetings. Especially when we were invited to pray and minister to the pastors and their guests. It was such a fun and exciting time to be a servant of the Lord!

My first time praying with the Haitians, I was partnered with Christy from Oklahoma. It was also my first time praying with someone using an interpreter. The experience was enlightening and encouraging. Holy Spirit healed EVERYONE we touched! Language didn't matter! People were healed from headaches, back pain, stomachaches, knee pain, hip pain, etc. Some of them had been struggling with their ailments since the earthquake four years before, and He healed them all!

The last person we prayed for that day was a little eight year-old girl who told Christy and me, through the interpreter, that her chest hurt. My first instinct was to think that this child was attention seeking, that she had just made up this complaint so she could be prayed for by the Americans. How sad is that? Pretty sad if you ask me - I cannot stand it when my emergency nursing mindset kicks in while I'm trying to minister to someone. Anyway, it should not have mattered WHY she came for prayer. She was looking for an encounter with God and Christy and I were chosen by the Holy Spirit to grant that desire of her heart.

However, when I placed my hand on her chest, I could FEEL her heart pounding against my hand! Let me tell you, my eyes got big and MY heart began to race. Not only could I feel that heart pounding (and I shouldn't have been able to), but it was racing. My mind went straight back into the natural and I could feel the fear crowding around me. I began praying over her, cursing the spirits of trauma and pain and commanding them to leave in the name of Jesus, but that heart kept pounding! I commanded the heart to return to a normal rate and strength in the name of Jesus and for the chest pain to leave. Still, nothing happened. We prayed against infection and inflammation and still nothing! What else could we do, but keep on praying. The longer her condition remained unchanged, the more concerned I became.

Eddie, one of the leaders on the team, came over and cast out the spirit of guilt. He said many of the survivors of the earthquake struggled with survivor's guilt, but that didn't work either. Then, He walked away! AHHHHHH! He walked away! I was starting to freak out on the inside. Something was seriously wrong with this little girl, yet I didn't know what it was. My anxiety was rising every minute this situation remained unresolved.

After another 10 minutes or so of continuously praying, Eddie walked back over and said, "*I just saw parasites drop off her in the spirit realm.*"

I let out a long breath and immediately relaxed. Holy Spirit whispered to me that what Eddie had said was indeed correct. Christy and I were able to focus our prayers on this parasite. We cursed any and ALL parasites in the mighty name of Jesus and commanded them to be removed from her body! The Holy Spirit then whispered to me to place my hand over her heart and to place HER hand over MY heart and to command HER heart to get into rhythm with mine.

Then it happened! Her heart stopped pounding and it returned to a normal rate! When you see healing come through your hands, you KNOW that you have encountered the Holy Spirit! What else could it have been?

Yes, I know. You may find THAT experience hard to believe, but it happened! The Holy Spirit is alive, desires to heal, and LOVES each and every one of us. We just need to humble ourselves and get out of His way so He can do His thing!

****

While there were plenty of opportunities to minister to the Haitians while we were in Haiti, we were also blessed with times where we could minister to each other. These times with each other, built eternal bonds between us that can never be broken. How blessed I feel to have built such strong, lasting friendships with people who were meant to be in my life as blessings, but also that I could hopefully bless in return.

One evening after dinner, I wandered back upstairs and found myself in a room shared by five amazing women whom I love and cherish. During this particular visit, I was able to spend some time with Leslie and Barb from Chicago. We had talked earlier in the day about seeing into the spirit realm and about how much I wanted to be able to see into the spirit realm and walk in the gift of discerning of spirits. They asked me if I had ever seen into the spirit realm and I answered, "*Sort of - on occasion.*"

They told me, "*No problem! Now it's going to increase!*" You see, they both walk in that particular gifting and they were going to impart it to me!

Leslie began by sharing the entire second chapter of 2 Kings with me. This particular scripture is about Elisha receiving a double portion of Elijah's anointing.

After reading the passage, she explained to me that the Lord had instructed her to share it with me prior to praying over me. As she and Barb prayed for me, they imparted the gift of discerning of spirits and the ability to see into the spirit realm. They cast out doubt and fear and just spoke amazing blessings over me. It was so edifying, encouraging, and uplifting when they reminded me that I am dearly and deeply loved and that I hold a very special place in Father God's heart.

They also told me, that my feet were anointed and would be guided by the Lord. Then, they asked me if I knew that I was very prophetic and had anyone ever told me that before. Strangely enough, I told them that three other people from three different organizations had told me that very same thing. They made four and five. They also released a greater anointing of healing and told me that my right hand was on fire, but, they cautioned me to guard my eyes and ears and my mind AND that my imagination was no longer human, but supernatural. They also warned me about talking myself out of what I was seeing, hearing, smelling, and experiencing. God was indeed trying to communicate with me, and I needed to be more diligent than ever in my response to that communication. So much goodness, so much impartation, so much revelation! *"God IS taking me to another level,"* I wrote in my journal. Thank You, Jesus!

You may be wondering how I can include this experience with Leslie and Barbara as an encounter with the Holy Spirit. Well, I have had follow-up experiences that confirm to me that I did, in fact encounter the Holy Spirit.

The first experience happened a little later that evening when I was visiting with Sally and Teresa in their room. I was standing in the middle of the room between their beds. Sally was on one side and Teresa was on the other. As I was looking out the window, I saw a brief flash of light far across the way. Barbara had cautioned me to be inquisitive and to ask God about EVERYTHING I was experiencing or noticing in the natural. So, upon seeing that flash of light, I asked Holy Spirit if that was Him and if so, what was it? He told me that it was Him and that He was just trying to get my attention. How cool is that?

It would have been so easy to talk myself out of that, but I was determined not to do that. I wanted to receive ALL that God had for me, so I can give it to all I come in contact with.

The second experience that proved I had encountered the Holy Spirit happened the next day while we were worshipping during the Pastor's conference. While I was singing and trying to connect with the Lord, Holy Spirit took me to a completely white room with a small marble table in the center. On the table was a small gift, wrapped in shiny red paper and bound with a beautiful shiny gold ribbon. He looked into my eyes and smiled warmly as He told me that the gift was for me.

I quietly asked, "*What is it?*" as I kept staring at this small, beautifully wrapped package sitting in the middle of the table. I couldn't take my eyes off of it; nor could I believe it was really for me!

He said, "*You have to open it. It's very small, but powerful. When you open it, you have to place it immediately into your mouth.*"

As strange as I thought that was, I just asked Him, "*Do I need to chew it?*"

He laughed and said, "*No. Just put it into your mouth and it will know what to do.*"

So, I carefully unwrapped the gift and found a small, glowing ball about the size of a golf ball. I didn't spend even one second looking at it as I popped it into my mouth as Holy Spirit had directed. The little glowing ball took off and traveled all over my body → to my eyes, to my brain, to my ears - EVERYWHERE!

As the glowing ball slowed to a stop, I asked Holy Spirit, "*What WAS that?*"

He responded with, "*That's the gift of discernment you asked for. Now, you have received it and I will show you over the next few weeks and months how to use it!*"

It's actually continued to grow over the past few years. It is wonderful to be in such a relationship with Holy Spirit! You have to try it sometime!

The third confirmation that my experience with Leslie and Barb was an encounter with the Holy Spirit occurred the following morning.

As we were traveling from the mission home to the church on the second day of the Pastor's conference, Holy Spirit told me that even though we had a security team in the natural to help keep us safe, we also had a supernatural security team. It was made up of four fifteen-foot angels that were positioned at the four corners of where ever we were. During our bus trips, they were positioned on the four corners of the roof of the bus. I thought that was pretty cool and somewhat exciting. I longed to actually see one of them. I wasn't privileged to see them that time around, but I did get to witness their actions in the natural.

The next evening as we were traveling to the church for the first night of the crusade, we came upon a soccer game being held in the middle of the street with makeshift goal posts. Our driver, Mano, demanded that they stop their game and move their goal posts so that we could pass through. The players were not interested in stopping their game and demanded that we drive around and/or find another way. They began walking towards us, swinging sticks and pipes as if they were planning to attack our bus. One guy even snarled at us just outside my window (I couldn't help but laugh)! However, within 30 seconds, those guys were moving the goal posts out of the way. It was awesome! I really believe that they caught a glimpse of our supernatural security team as they jumped down from the bus to "help encourage" them to move out of the way. Seriously! There was no reason for them to stop their attack on us, and it was over before it even started.

The fourth experience that confirmed my encounter with the Holy Spirit while I was being prayed over by Leslie and Barbara occurred on our very last night in the country. It was the evening of Easter Sunday and this was our last service to minister to the people of Haiti. It was a long and exhausting week, but so rewarding to be a part of what God was doing to rebuild this country after the devastating earthquake in January 2010. We started the evening service like every other service and that was with a prolonged period of worship, except THIS time was different!

Worship was incredible! I wish I could share with you the videos that we took of the Haitians worshipping God with such joy, love, excitement, and expectation. We danced, sang, worshipped, and praised Him for well over an hour! It was such a privilege to be there. They taught US what worship was supposed to look like. It was 95 degrees with 95% humidity and we were all jumping around for Jesus. WHAT a celebration we were having! The Holy Spirit didn't have a choice but to show up.

The music ended and everyone took their seats in anticipation of what was going to happen next. Pastor Marcus, from our team, got up and began his presentation on the baptism of the Holy Spirit. Ten minutes into his sermon, I noticed a commotion off to my right and someone began yelling, "*We need a nurse over here!*" I jumped up from my seat and rushed over to the right corner of the room to find a young girl lying unresponsive on the ground.

My first thought was that she was suffering from the heat - maybe heat exhaustion or something worse like heat stroke. As I made my initial assessment of this young lady, I soon discovered that she had a strong, bounding pulse that was regular, not tachycardic (rapid) as I would anticipate someone who was suffering from the heat. Plus, her breathing was even and unlabored, her skin was NOT hot to the touch, nor was she sweating - ALL contraindications to my initial assessment of a heat related emergency.

With heat stroke and/or heat exhaustion, we have a very serious condition that requires immediate medical attention. The most common signs and symptom usually include skin temperature above 105 degrees, rapid heartbeat, nausea, and a severe headache. Other symptoms may or may not include dizziness and fainting, extreme fatigue, vomiting, mental confusion, seizures, lack of sweating, and severe headache, most of which I could not ascertain because the young woman was unresponsive. I'm rapidly thinking about what else could possibly be going on, and then I knew. This wasn't a physical problem, but a spiritual one.

I was in a conundrum. What was I supposed to do? The battle within myself was fierce! My nurse side of me wanted to stay in the natural to resolve the problem, but my spirit knew beyond a shadow of a doubt that this was spiritual. The worst part of this for me was I had NO idea what to do, so I just began praying in the Spirit using my personal prayer language! Within minutes, Courtney, one of our other nurses showed up beside me and asked me what was going on and how could she help. As soon as I let her know this was spiritual, she began commanding and rebuking everything that came to her mind. While she was speaking, I reached down and lifted the young woman's eyelids and they remained open! Yikes!

"*Ok, that's not good,*" I initially thought. Then, I looked into her eyes and saw snake's eyes looking back at me! (You know, the eyes with the vertical, elliptical pupils). That's when Barbara, another one of our nurses on the team, came up behind me and began praying in the Spirit.

So, we have Courtney commanding and rebuking, Barb was praying in the spirit and I began speaking directly to the spirit I believed was manifesting through this young woman. I told it that we knew it was there and it WAS going to come out! Right after I said that, another woman began having an asthma attack a few feet away and Barbara had to leave to take care of her.

Thankfully, it was a minor issue just requiring the woman to use her inhaler and Barbara was able to return to help once again. When she began praying again, the young woman's body began to "*slither*" on the ground like a snake. No joke! I don't know how else to describe it, but as soon as she did that, I knew right away that we were dealing with -- a spirit of python!

I began shouting, "*It's a spirit of python! It's a spirit of python!*"

Barbara intensified her praying in the spirit and Courtney and I began cursing the spirit of python and commanding it to come out of her in the name of Jesus and by the power of the Holy Spirit! I had learned in previous training with my friend Libby from Deep Water Ministries that we needed to cut the spirit of python into seven pieces in the spirit realm and the person had to cough, belch, sigh, etc., seven times to indicate that each piece had been removed. Otherwise, if only a part of this demon was removed, it could easily grow back and be ten times as strong and more difficult to remove.

So, after I sliced up that demon in the spirit realm, we commanded together that it needed to come out of her right now, in the name of Jesus! We did it over and over. The young woman really began writhing on the floor, but she coughed! Once, twice, three times! She opened her eyes, coughed again for a fourth time and then she sat up.

Everyone around us was cheering and shouting and pushing in, trying to get as close as they could. Our interpreter, Gabriel, was ecstatic! He was so excited to be helping us, to be helping the Holy Spirit deliver this young lady, but I told him to tell her we were not finished! She still needed to cough three more times!

Gabriel said, "*No, she says she is feeling alright.*"

I said, "*No! She has to cough three more times. She has not completely been delivered yet.*" So, everyone kept praying, shouting, commanding, and rebuking! Finally, she coughed three more times and ended with one long sigh. Now, I KNEW that demon had been completely expelled!

We talked with her, asking her questions, making sure she was ok to get up before we assisted her to her feet. Once we determined that she was only 16 years of age, we made sure there was an adult who was going to assume responsibility for her before allowing her to leave. It was also a great comfort to learn that she attended the local Christian academy and would have plenty of support in preventing this demon from trying to get back in.

Some of you reading this right now will doubt that this actually occurred. I can assure you, it did. As I have stated before, you might be able to doubt or question my theology, but you cannot take away my experience.

The Holy Spirit loved that young woman so much that He wanted her to be free! Free to be who He created her to be. He loved ME so much, that He allowed ME to participate in this deliverance. First by discerning that the spirit of python was manifesting, then, by guiding us through her deliverance. There is no way we would have EVER been able to do that without Him!

Now, just in case you forgot, this manifestation occurred while Pastor Marcus was teaching on the Baptism of the Holy Spirit. This demon was trying to do whatever it could to keep Marcus from teaching that lesson, but it failed! When we were able to return to our seats, we learned that over 200 Haitians had received the Baptism of the Holy Spirit while we were "assisting" the Holy Spirit with the young girl's deliverance! God is so good and I feel so blessed!

The important thing about this particular chapter is learning that Holy Spirit is always moving. He wants to touch the lives of as many people as possible and He chooses His children to do that. We have to be willing AND available. Just say, "*Yes*!" Because when you say, "*Yes*," you will have the privilege of bringing Holy Spirit's touch to a hurting world. You will have the honor of seeing someone else's life change just like your life was changed. I encourage you to become a willing vessel. Ask Holy Spirit to use you, because when you DO, I promise, He WILL!

THE IMPORTANT THING ABOUT THIS PARTICULAR CHAPTER IS LEARNING THAT HOLY SPIRIT IS ALWAYS MOVING.

Choosing to serve the Holy Spirit in Haiti was like being thrown into the deep end of the pool. Never in a million years did I expect to experience the Holy Spirit the way I did. The weeks prior to this trip, He kept telling me that this trip wasn't about the Haitians. It was about me, but through the gifts He gave to me, the Haitians were abundantly blessed.

I didn't choose to share those experiences with you to brag about all that Holy Spirit did in and through me. I chose to share them with you because I believe, deep inside of myself, that if He did it for me, He will indeed, do it for you. You don't have to worry about Holy Spirit forcing you to do or be anything you don't want to do or be. He is THE perfect gentleman and NEVER forces Himself upon anyone and will never force anyone to do anything they don't want to do. However, He does and will act accordingly when invited to do so.

You have to understand that I had been asking Holy Spirit to reveal Himself to me, and to become more and more involved in my life for years. Little did I know, He was actively working in the background of my life all that time to bring about the experiences I just shared with you. So, when it seems like nothing is happening, when it seems like you ask and ask and ask for something and it never comes, rest assured, it IS coming and it will knock your spiritual socks off! All you have to do is to be open to all that the Holy Spirit has for you and receive it unto yourself!

Chapter Nineteen

Entering In

"Blessed are the pure in heart for they will see God."
~ Matthew 5:8

Earlier in this book, I wrote about some prayer ministry that I experienced with my friend Sally at Living Faith Church. She led me through some amazing things when I first started meeting with her, so every now and then I am led to check in with her.

This time I made an appointment and we just began talking about everything that was going on and getting caught up. It had been quite a while since we had worked on things, so there was a LOT to talk about!

Somehow, we got to talking about how I would cope with things before I accepted Jesus as my Lord and Savior. I shared how I could just sit down at my keyboard and just get lost in the music. Whenever I was upset, sad, excited, depressed, overwhelmed, or whatever; I would sit down and put ALL of that emotion into the music. When I was finished, I felt like a new person and better equipped to deal with whatever I was struggling with.

When I mentioned this to Sally, her eyes sparkled as she asked me if I thought Jesus might have been there. I told her I didn't think so, but she disagreed. So, she said, *"Let's ask Him."* So, we did! She led me in asking Jesus if He was there and He said, *"Absolutely."*

I asked Him, *"Where were you, then? Show me."*

He brought me into the most beautiful scene. There I was, sitting at the keyboard playing and He just casually walks up and asks me, "*May I join you?*"

Sheepishly, I said, "*Yes, Please!*"

He sat down beside me on the piano bench and started playing the keyboard with me. It started out slow and then sped up, both of our hands and arms intertwining as we played some of the most beautiful music that I had ever heard. We laughed, sang, and just enjoyed each other's company. This was a time that I could honestly say that I felt the joy of the Lord! Nothing else mattered. All was well in my world! I didn't have to think about anything but Him and the music. It was such a healing balm to my soul.

As the vision began to fade from my view, Sally exclaimed, "*What a beautiful picture! Now, you can go there, anytime that you want, and share this same experience with Him!*"

She was right! I have used this many times since then to enter into His presence.

Wow! I was and am blessed beyond words. My Lord and Savior enjoys the same things I do and loves to do them with me. Who would have thought that something so basic and so simple could bring healing to my soul? You know, you can do that, too! Find something that you enjoy and picture Jesus doing it with you. Make it your happy place and before you know it, you will be experiencing HIS joy all the time, too!

As my visit with Sally continued, another picture came to my mind. This time I was in prison, a cage to be more exact. While I was looking out through the steel bars, Jesus walked up and unlocked the door to the prison. Even with the door wide open, I didn't know that I could leave the cage. The cage was home. It felt normal. Actually, it felt rather safe and comfortable. I couldn't remember what it was like outside of the cage. Fear ravaged my heart at the thought of leaving my surroundings, but, oh, how I desired to do just that. I mean, Jesus was just on the other side. However, I had to CHOOSE to step out of that cage.

Jesus kept inviting me to come out, but I didn't think I could. He didn't give up, though. He kept inviting me to join Him outside of the cage. "*Come on, Rachel. Come here! It's better than you remember*," He kept telling me.

I finally got a little courage and put one foot out, touching outside the cage as if I would be zapped or something and rapidly pulling my foot back in.

Jesus smiled when He said, "*See, nothing happened. Why don't you come a little further? Come on. I'm right here. You are safe in My arms. I will protect you. Trust me. You will find that I am MORE than faithful.*"

At that point, I gained a little more courage and I stepped outside the cage with both feet, but immediately jumped back inside as if I was expecting something bad to happen. Now, you have to realize that the door remained open the entire time and I was free to come and go as I wanted, but I just didn't believe it. How sad is that?

After a few more episodes of jumping in and out the door, I took one giant step and reached for Jesus' hand. He grabbed it and pulled me into a full body hug. I was enveloped by Him, encircled by His arms and more importantly by His love. He loved on me and reminded me that I was safe and that He would never leave me nor forsake me. This time, I believed Him. There was no doubt. It cannot exist in His arms or in His presence.

His embrace was wonderful and He allowed me to stay there for as long as I wanted. When I was ready, we began walking down the street, talking, sharing, and holding hands. Yep! A relationship with Jesus is just that simple and just that normal.

That's the kind of relationship He wants to have with every one of us.

Now, that I was safely outside of that cage, Jesus reached over, picked it up and held it between both of His hands. After a few seconds, He smashed it until it was a powder lying on the ground at His feet. I watched in amazement as I wondered what that could mean. Immediately He spoke and said, *"Rachel, that cage no longer has any power over you. I have broken all ties to it for all eternity. You are free!"*

Deep inside, I knew that was true. The thing the cage represented no longer had a hold on me and never would again. This is true freedom. When Jesus says you are free, you are free, indeed! (John 8:36)

We then began walking down the street again. He was on my right side and I began to wonder if that mattered. This is when I began to notice the row of cages that were lined up along that side of the street. He had positioned Himself between me and those cages.

So, I asked Him, *"Why? Don't you trust me?"*

He responded, *"Rachel, I am your Protector, your Healer, your Provider. THAT is My job! I chose you and you chose me! It brings me great joy to encircle you in My love and keep you safe."*

He continued, *"Could I protect you from your left side? Absolutely! But I want to keep you from even the slightest temptation. Let's switch sides for a moment so you can see."*

We switched sides. He was now walking on my left and I was walking on His right. Not only could I see all of the cages, but I could hear ALL of the voices! Some were begging me to help them to get out, too. While others were trying to draw me in, reminding me of my time in the cage. After only a minute of that, I asked Him if we could switch back and He said, *"Certainly!"* I really didn't like being that exposed and preferred to be secure in His presence.

Walking down the street with Jesus like that was very real. It was very freeing and it built within me a sense of safety, a sense of freedom, and a sense of belonging to Him. My life was changed once again by spending time in His presence.

After that session with Sally, I no longer felt bogged down by worry, anxiety, or depression. It's a feeling that is difficult to describe. I felt joy from deep inside of me and I didn't have any reason except that I was in His presence and safely tucked under the shadow of His wings (Psalms 17:8, 91:4).

That kind of freedom changes you. When you are able to release all of your worries, concerns, and weaknesses to Him, you live differently. You respond to situations differently. I started developing a boldness I had not experienced before, a confidence that I had not felt before, and a desire to be in His presence all of the time. You see, an encounter with the Godhead changes you. That's how you know it's real! You don't have to work at it or even think about. It just happens.

So, you might be wondering or even asking, "*How can I enter into God's presence?*" I remember back in my second year at the Ministry Training Center, Bebette asked us that very question. "*How do YOU enter into God's presence?*" I had no idea. I didn't even really understand what she was asking me, to be perfectly honest with you. "*God's presence? Who has EVER been there but Moses, Jesus, and the apostles?*"

You see, we make it more difficult than it needs to be. Remember, everything about the gospel is simple. EVERYTHING!

It starts with our imagination. Yes, you read that correctly, our imaginations were created by God and given to us so He could effectively communicate with us. Unfortunately, for most of us, we were instructed at a very young age to turn off or shut down our imaginations. Who was ever told by a teacher or even a parent to "***Stop that daydreaming and pay attention?***" Even though I don't have any recollection of the event, I'm sure at some point I was. I know because it took me a long time to be able to use my imagination again.

YOUR IMAGE CENTER OR IMAGINATION WILL HELP YOU SEE GOD IN SPECIAL WAYS.

What I would like to encourage you to do, is start to see your imagination as your image center. It's like a big white board created by God to display pictures in your mind. Your image center or imagination will help you see God in special ways.

Matthew 5:8 says, "*Blessed are the pure in heart for they will see God.*"

The enemy (satan) doesn't want us to see or encounter God because He knows how it will strengthen and build us up. He wants to take our imagination from us! Why? Because, He came to steal, kill, and destroy (John 10:10) anything that will bring us closer to God.

You're probably not going to like this, but I am going to take you somewhere that you may not be happy about. I'm going to show you how satan tries to mess with your imagination.

Do you like paranormal movies? How about violent ones? Maybe you are into porn or murder mysteries. Basically, anything that isn't good, lovely, or of good rapport, will mess with your imagination (Philippians 4:8). These pictures become imbedded in our imaginations and they make everything messy. They

BASICALLY, ANYTHING THAT ISN'T GOOD, LOVELY, OR OF GOOD RAPPORT, WILL MESS WITH YOUR IMAGINATION.

bring on bad dreams, scary thoughts, and haunted images. It's the reason why we run up the stairs really fast because we feel like something scary is chasing us or we leap from the doorway onto our bed, so the "monster under the bed" won't get us. How many of you have to sleep with the closet door shut? I think you get the idea.

It's because our imaginations have been messed with and now they are messed up. Some of the things we see in our dysfunctional families, like children being abused, parents having sex, drinking alcohol, or doing drugs can mess with our imaginations. Now before you get yourself feeling like a lost cause, let me remind you that the gospel is and has always been GOOD NEWS! God has equipped the Holy Spirit with a giant eraser to clean up our imaginations!

Put your hand on your forehead and repeat this prayer.

Come, Holy Spirit. I ask You to come and clean my image center. I ask You to forgive me and wash away all of the bad things that I chose to put into my imagination. Please return my imagination to a clean and safe place for You to draw Your pictures. Thank You, Holy Spirit, for giving me an imagination. I choose to honor it and ask You to help me to keep it clean. Holy Spirit, right now, I ask You to replace the bad images with something from the Word of God. Amen.

Now I want you to watch and see what Jesus does. This is a big deal to have your imagination cleaned up! It's not a small thing! You should clean it up as often as you can.

Now I want you to say, "*MY imagination is ready for God to draw His pictures on it*!"

God is the ultimate dreamer. The devil has tricked many people by telling us that our imaginations are silly, not real, or even foolish, but the reality is that our imagination is a gift from God. It can be used for God's glory. When you surrender your image center to God, He will cleanse it, transform it, and use it for His purposes. Just imagine what a clean and God-focused imagination can do!

God wants us to dream His dreams. He wants us to experience His Kingdom, and He loves to reveal it to us through pictures in our imaginations.

Put your hand over your eyes and read this prayer.

Thank You Jesus for giving me eyes to see You. Come now and breathe life and truth into my imagination (Picture Jesus breathing on your imagination). Help me to see Your pictures. Draw your thoughts into my mind.

Now take a moment to see if the Holy Spirit will bring something to your image center. Did you get anything?

I know it can seem silly or even unspiritual, but as you look at these pictures through HIS eyes and HIS mind, you are going to discover aspects of Him that you didn't know.

Pray this prayer.

Holy Spirit, You are good and You promised that if we call out to You, You would answer us. So, Lord, right now, I come to You, and say that I want You to speak to me. I want to hear Your voice. I choose to silence my own thoughts right now. I quiet my mind. I declare that this is a safe place and I refuse all the lies of the enemy in Jesus' name. I choose to only hear Your voice. Holy Spirit, would You come and speak into my heart, right now? Thank You, Lord, Amen!

Pay attention to what you are feeling, sensing, and hearing. Be open and encounter God in a new and amazing way. He has so much to show you!

Chapter Twenty

My New Coat

"The Spirit Himself bears witness with our spirit that we are children of God, and if children, then heirs—heirs of God and joint heirs with Christ, if indeed we suffer with Him, that we may also be glorified together." ~ Romans 8:16-17

One Sunday, after church, I participated in an event known as a Sozo. Sozo is the Greek word defined as "healing" (Matthew 9:22 - well = Sozo), "salvation" (Romans 10:9 - saved = Sozo), and "deliverance" (Luke 8:36 - well = Sozo). The purpose of a Sozo is to help you get to the root of anything that is interfering with your connection to the Father, Jesus, and/or the Holy Spirit. Once this connection is healed, you are able to walk out your destiny. A team of two or three meets with you and guides you into interactions with the Godhead that leads you to freedom and wholeness. It's not counseling, but another avenue to assist you into encounters with Father God, Jesus, and the Holy Spirit.

In this particular Sozo session, we were dealing with guilt and shame. I'm thinking that almost everybody deals with that during a Sozo at one point or another. Anyway, we discovered many lies that I had been believing. We had gotten to the part of exchanging the lie with something Father God wanted to give to me in return. That's when Holy Spirit showed me my new coat! It was absolutely spectacular! One of the most beautiful coats I had EVER seen (and that's saying a LOT because clothes/coats do not excite me). It was kind of like what I imagined the coat of many colors that Joseph wore back in the Old Testament (Genesis 37), but much more breathtakingly beautiful! The colors were so vibrant and sparkly. I didn't even recognize all of the colors and there were all kinds of different jewels all over the coat!

He wanted ME to give Him, my dirty, tattered coat, first. He told me that the old, dirty, nasty coat represented the shame, guilt, worthlessness, and lack of value that I had been wearing most of my life. Now, He would replace it with THIS new coat that represented my true worth and value, but I could only have it if I gave Him the old one. Let me just tell you, I was at a time in my life when I was really searching for my true identity – the person God intended me to be. So, I was more than ready to give Him that old coat filled with guilt and shame, worthlessness and lacking value. I could NOT get it off fast enough. I didn't really care if I had a new coat, to tell you the truth; I just really wanted to get rid of the old one! I knew right away that this coat represented my true identity.

I handed Him the old coat. He didn't grab it. He just kind of enveloped it and then it disappeared. Then, Holy Spirit invited me to turn around as He gently slipped my new coat up over both my arms at the same time and onto my shoulders. I wrapped it around myself and just began twirling, enjoying the beauty and the love that I felt from that coat. While I was twirling, I could hear Holy Spirit laughing and could feel the love just pouring out of Him.

When I finally finished twirling, He said, "*You look marvelous! It looks really good on you, like it was meant to be there your entire life (because it was)!*" Then He lifted me up onto His lap, lifted my chin to look at Him, and said,

"*THIS is a coat that all of My children wear. I want you to honor and value it and always remember that you are MORE than worth it and your value exceeds anything on this planet, including this coat. The identity that you found in that old coat was never meant for you. I want you to forget about that old identity and fully engage with this new identity, your true identity. The identity you were meant to have when I created you. YOU are beautiful just the way you are! You are everything that I ever wanted you to be!"*

It amazes me every time I think about it. To think, that identity, that coat, was mine and I had held onto that old, nasty coat for 41 years! Now, I'm just excited to learn how to walk with this new coat and live life as I was originally created to do!

The Bible shows us so many things about ourselves. Each time we read it, or at least each time I read it, I find myself identifying with someone in there. Most of the time I tend to identify with King David, always striving to have a heart like Jesus, but struggling with the choices I make in my life. Maybe you might find yourself identifying with Ruth or Esther or maybe Peter or Paul. Whoever we choose, we do so because their lives are similar to our own. How many of us choose Jesus as the person we identify with, the person we choose to model our lives after?

The truth is, we aren't called to become like anyone BUT Jesus. Think about that! If we never model our lives after Jesus, then something is terribly wrong here! God wants us to become more like Him, not Paul, Esther, Ruth, or King David. If we desire to be "made into His image", we need to start identifying ourselves with Him. Jesus must become our role model and be allowed to live His life through us.

The good news is God is in love with us! He is the only person Who can lead us into discovering who He really created us to be! His work begins on the inside, which will forever change our outside behavior in a real and tangible way. His love for us personally, will change us. It will help us identify ourselves as children of God. The more we understand who we are and Whose we are, the greater the power of His kingdom will manifest through us. Everything about

HE IS THE ONLY PERSON WHO CAN LEAD US INTO DISCOVERING WHO HE REALLY CREATED US TO BE!

THE KEY TO OPERATING IN THE POWER OF GOD IS KNOWING OUR IDENTITY IN CHRIST.

walking in signs, miracles, and wonders begins with our level of understanding of our identity. The key to operating in the power of God is knowing our identity in Christ and how He wants to work in and through us.

When you discover that, your life will never be the same! I am here to tell you that since Holy Spirit blessed me with this vision of "my coat", my life has never been the same. I carry myself differently - my head held high and my shoulders squared. There's no fear in looking somebody directly in the eye or sharing the gospel or even my opinions with others, because I know He has my back.

Because of this new coat, I realized that my walk with the Holy Spirit was now going to drastically change. The Bible teaches us in Romans 8:14 that,

> *"those who are led by the Spirit of God are the sons of God."*

When you are truly walking with the Holy Spirit, life takes on a new flow where there is no striving. I learned how to rest in the arms of Jesus and how to let Him dictate the path that was best for me. There was no longer any need to strive to make my place in the family of God because I was already a part of it. I just didn't know it.

Now, when the Holy Spirit presents me with a key to open a door to a new opportunity, I don't have to spend time thinking and worrying about it. I just put the key in, open the door, and walk through.

You see, the reason Sozo really works is because it exposes lies you have been believing your whole life and replaces them with truth. When this happens, those lies can never deceive or control you again because they no longer define who you are. The devil deceives people by whispering lies about who they are. He gains access to us through pain and/or trauma and then plants these lies in our minds. These lies create a hot mess in our lives, our circumstances, and our relationships. Every work of the devil is based on lies. Don't believe me? Look at what John 8:44 has to say.

> *"You are of your father the devil, and the desires of your father you want to do. He was a murderer from the beginning, and does not stand in the truth, because there is no truth in him. When he speaks a lie, he speaks from his own resources,* **for he is a liar and the father of it.**"(emphasis added)

We will begin to walk in all that Jesus promised us, when the lies are exposed and removed from our minds by the Holy Spirit. Holy Spirit "power washes" our minds and we begin to receive revelation about who we REALLY are. When that happens, all the hindrances that we have been struggling against just fall away and we begin to walk in all that God has called us to be and do.

There are so many believers who have been slimed by the devil and are not walking in the abundant life that Jesus died to give them. They are struggling to have intimacy with God that can only be found in His presence. But you know what? Those outside of the circle called believers are desperate for freedom, too (Romans 8:21). Their freedom depends on ours. Therefore, it's really important that believers DO NOT believe the lie that becoming a Christian only promises access to heaven. It's so much more than that!

Believers shift the atmosphere by breaking their allegiance with the father of lies and choosing to align with the almighty Creator. When we do that, we learn to reign as kings and queens. We learn how to bring heaven to earth just like Jesus taught (Matthew 6:9-10).

BELIEVERS SHIFT THE ATMOSPHERE BY BREAKING THEIR ALLEGIANCE WITH THE FATHER OF LIES AND CHOOSING TO ALIGN WITH THE ALMIGHTY CREATOR.

Jesus came to destroy the works of the devil (1 John 3:8) and when He left, He sent the Holy Spirit to help us to do the same (John 14:16). He is free to function as directed when we have our true identities revealed to us. Do you know who you really are in Christ? Are you living in the freedom only the children of God know? Are you living on the earth as Jesus did, destroying the works of the enemy and declaring the Father? Be encouraged. As you uncover lie after lie, you WILL change and as YOU change, you WILL change the world!

Chapter Twenty-One

Soaking

"Meditate within your heart on your bed, and be still."
~ Psalm 4:4

This chapter may just be the most important chapter in the entire book! To me, it ties everything together and shows how to press into and grow in the things of God. I'm not talking about gaining knowledge - anyone can gain knowledge. I have an extensive library, three degrees and a diploma from a four-year Ministry Training Center, but that's not what I'm talking about.

When we talk about intimacy with God - it's not about getting "born again." Yes, getting "born again" SHOULD lead us on a path of getting intimate with God, but it doesn't always. Why? Because there isn't a whole lot of teaching on it. Today's church isn't really teaching how to be intimate with God. What they are giving us is knowledge. It's what we choose to do with that knowledge that makes the difference. We need to realize that when we get intimate with God, He gets ALL over us, and that's what we take with us as we go into the world.

> **WE NEED TO REALIZE THAT WHEN WE GET INTIMATE WITH GOD, HE GETS ALL OVER US, AND THAT'S WHAT WE TAKE WITH US AS WE GO INTO THE WORLD.**

Growing in the things of God means that I am able to take the Word of God and the truth of the Word of God, build it into my life, and live it out in everyday situations.

The alternative to growing in the things of God is knowledge. A lot of us have gained knowledge, but if that knowledge remains just knowledge, with no fruit or out working in our lives, then that knowledge will not bring us into intimacy with God.

Let's take a moment and imagine that you own a company or that you are the hiring manager for a company. You have two candidates for a position that you want to hire for. The first candidate is a recent graduate of a major university, has earned his MBA, but has zero work experience. Your second candidate does not have ANY degrees, but has been working in a similar job for another company over the past 15 years. Which candidate do you think you would choose if they were both equal in every other category?

Most of us would choose the candidate with experience.

WE'VE LEARNED THE VERSES, WE'VE LEARNED THE PRINCIPLES, AND WE'VE LEARNED THE THEOLOGY, BUT WE'RE NOT DOING IT!

There's one thing in life that we cannot buy and that's experience. You have to live it! I want us, as Christians, to get to a place, where we are not just talking about this stuff. We've learned the verses, we've learned the principles, and we've learned the theology, but we're not doing it! As the church, as the bride of Christ, we are NOT living what we know. We are NOT living out of His presence. We have to get that experience with Him!

I really want us to come to an understanding of the need for this foundational experience with God. We have to be able to take the Word of God, understand how faith works, put it into practice and see it work! Whether it's laying hands on the sick, delivering a person, or praying over a situation and watching it turn around, we NEED to learn to experience God and experience Him individually.

My experience with God is not going to be the same as your experience with God. There's a reason for that. I'm glad that it's that way. We are NOT cookie-cutters or cookie cutouts. God is big and we make the mistake of putting him into a box. That's not how God works. We need to have our own experience with Him.

I can worship God in a way that warms my heart and warms His heart because I am the only Rachel expression of God on the earth! YOU are the only YOU expression of God on the earth. Isn't that beautiful? We were ALL created in His image, but for different things.

So, right now, I want to talk about getting into His presence because that's where heaven meets earth. That's where everything changes. That's where the fruit is cultivated. That's where we learn how to be the tool in the master's hand to bring change to other people's lives. That's where we help others to meet Jesus. One of the tools I like to use to help me get into the presence of God is called soaking. It's using music to help set the atmosphere for an intimate encounter with God. The first time, two, three, or four, you may wonder if God is really going to show up. Don't worry! He ALWAYS shows up! The more you press in, the more you seek Him, the more you will find Him (Jeremiah 29:13; Deuteronomy 4:29; Proverbs 8:17; Matthew 7:7-8; Hebrews 11:6). - He promises that in the Bible - because, He wants that, too!

The more time we spend with Him, the more we are going to recognize His voice, His smell, His touch, and His presence. So, the next time we are out in the world, we are going to know that He is right there walking with us. Even though our minds may know this, it's more important to know it in our hearts. Because that is when we will live our lives differently.

THE MORE TIME WE SPEND WITH HIM, THE MORE WE ARE GOING TO RECOGNIZE HIS VOICE, HIS SMELL, HIS TOUCH, AND HIS PRESENCE.

A lot of you reading this are already soaking and some of you need to be encouraged to do so. This is ME encouraging YOU to soak. It will CHANGE YOUR LIFE!

Most of us should be soaking every day, multiple times per day. It doesn't have to be particularly lengthy. God can do as much in five minutes as He can do in twenty or sixty minutes. It's our time to enjoy Him, asking Him WHO He is and how His day was. It's NOT a time to take our pressing needs, wants, and desires to Him. When we are soaking, we are spending time in the presence of God, so that our entire being - spirit, soul, and body are saturated in His presence (1 Thessalonians 5:23).

When I get into this place of soaking, I like to have my Bible, a notepad, and a pen. That way I can write down what God is saying to me right then. I don't want to miss a thing. This way I can go back and review what He is telling me OR if I am being distracted, I can write the distraction down and plan to take care of it AFTER my time with the Lord. This is how God's army is built. It's not built on knowledge, but the fruit of applying that knowledge - our experience with Him.

The most powerful leaders in the church like Smith Wigglesworth, John G. Lake, Kathryn Kuhlman, Charles & Francis Hunter, Joan Hunter, Katie Souza, Randy Clark, Bill Johnson, and many others - are able to be effective because of the time they spend in His presence. He reveals "great and mighty" things in His presence (Jeremiah 33:3). When you have that experience, nobody can take that away. They can take books away. They can take your Bible away, but they cannot take your experience with God away. NO ONE can take it away. No one can make you deny it. Nobody can make you doubt it because it's YOURS and it happened to you!

In the Webster's dictionary, SOAKING is defined as,

- To be immersed in liquid

- To become saturated by immersion

- To penetrate and/or affect the mind and feelings

- To fill thoroughly

Soaking can be synonymous with prolonged immersion and complete absorption. Other synonyms might include, to absorb, assimilate, marinate, permeate, and saturate. This gets me soooo excited because these words make the word, soaking, come alive.

So, what does soaking mean in the life of a believer?

It's time spent with God, allowing your entire heart (spirit), soul (mind, will, and emotions), and body to be immersed, saturated, permeated, penetrated, marinated, filled, and totally absorbed in His presence. Now, keep in mind that this is NOT a duty that you do because it's something God has required of you. That's legalistic. You don't do this to earn points with God. This is something that is pleasurable, something to be enjoyed. You just rest there and let God love on you. Let Him wrap His arms around you. Let Him drop revelation into your heart.

SOAKING IS TIME SPENT WITH GOD, ALLOWING YOUR ENTIRE HEART (SPIRIT), SOUL (MIND, WILL, AND EMOTIONS), AND BODY TO BE IMMERSED, SATURATED, PERMEATED, PENETRATED, MARINATED, FILLED, AND TOTALLY ABSORBED IN HIS PRESENCE.

Will He give you resolutions to your problems? Absolutely! Are you refrained from asking questions? Nope. He WANTS us to ask Him questions. He likes it when we come to Him and ask, "*But God, why this or why that?*" He wants us to understand Him and Who He is. We want people to know us, right? Our closest family and friends KNOW us, know why we behave the way we do, they know everything about us. God wants the same thing. He wants that same interaction, that same intimacy.

If you make this a "have to do it" kind of thing, you're not going to do it. However, if you see it as getting intimate with the God of all creation, I believe you will find yourself rushing to get into His presence.

God's intention from the beginning was that we would live in an intimate relationship with Him. The whole concept of the Garden of Eden before the fall was that it was a place of intimacy. Adam and Eve walked in the cool of the day with Him. Thanks to Jesus, His death on the cross and His resurrection, we can have the same kind of intimacy that Adam had with God before the fall.

Now, how do we soak? There are five steps to soaking:

1. **Create the atmosphere** (Make provision for possible distractions).

- Find a quiet place. Turn off the phone, television, computer, tablet, radio, mp3 player, etc. Dim the lights. Adjust the temperature of the room. Find some music that is soft, relaxing, and peaceful. Music moves us. It opens our abilities to be more inspired, to be able to see and hear God. Choose something quiet. Remember, it's an intimate time. Get your pen, paper, and your Bible. Put on some comfy clothes. Get your favorite comfy pillow and assume a position that is comfortable for you. You are putting yourself into a position to receive freely from Holy Spirit.

2. **You don't need to close your eyes.**

- It's not wrong to close your eyes, but it's not necessary. Some people choose to close them to block out visual distractions. However, you can sit looking out your window and meditate on God's creation and how each tree, bush, and cloud all represent God is some way or fashion.

A few years ago when I was spending some time with a close friend of mine in the country of Senegal. Every morning, I found myself sitting on the beach, listening to the crashing waves as I had quiet time with God. I didn't even realize I was soaking, but that wasn't important. What was important was that I was using God's creation to bring me into intimate moments with Him, moments that changed me and ones that I will never forget.

3. **Speak out loud**.

- Most of us are used to praying with our minds. There's nothing wrong with that. However, God wants to hear your voice and your mind NEEDS to hear your voice. It needs to hear you invite the Holy Spirit into this time, to lead and guide you (John 16:13). You might consider saying something like this; "*Holy Spirit, I invite You into this time. I welcome Your presence. Thank You for being here with me.*" Holy Spirit is a gentleman. He will never enter your life or your time un-invited, so you NEED to invite Him. Talk to Him using your mouth, not your mind. He DOES hear the prayers in your mind, but He wants you to use your words because He knows you benefit from hearing them. Don't be afraid. Holy Spirit will not lead you down the wrong path. He always leads us away from the darkness and into the light.

4. **Consciously turn your heart towards Jesus.**

- Picture His face. One of my favorite things to do is to picture myself crawling up onto Jesus' lap and letting Him wrap His arms around me. It wasn't always like that. A few years ago, I was visiting my friend Maria in South Korea when she recommended doing that in my quiet time with God. I really thought she was crazy. I didn't understand it at all, but I decided to give it a try and my prayer life has never been the same. Just focus on the different parts of Him. Be childlike. This is YOU looking for intimacy and it's a choice.

- Ask Him, "*How are you today, Jesus or Holy Spirit or Father God?*" Listen to what He says. Be prepared for Him to respond with the same question to you! Can you be honest with Him and tell Him exactly how you are feeling or will you allow an upset stomach or a stuffy nose keep you from this time with Him? It's during these times that He will explain to you how something in your past may be creating the current paradigm you are living in.

- Intentionally turn your affections to Him. "*Lord, it's been busy this morning. Oh, how I love You! Thank You Jesus! Thank You Holy Spirit for Your presence!*" You can do this ALL DAY LONG! By encountering God in this manner, He will respond because you are inviting Him into the situation.

Watch out for distractions. In the beginning you might be bombarded with tons of distractions, things you need to do or something you forgot to do. Write them down on your notepad and get to them later. Don't allow them to interfere with your time with Him. The enemy loves to distract us by getting us to focus on Him and not God (Psalm 68:2). The more we think about the problem, the bigger it gets. If we focus on God instead of the problem, the bigger God becomes, and eventually the problem will go away. The more time we spend in God's presence, the less time we will be spending on the devil's distractions.

There may be times when you will feel uncomfortable in His presence. A face might pop into your mind. Ask the Holy Spirit to show you the issue or anything else you might need to know. Ask Him for forgiveness for any sins that He brings to your mind. THEN, forgive yourself, and make it right with that person, if necessary. Of course, sometimes you just don't feel well and don't have the heart or the strength to soak with Him. It's not necessary to be at your best because:

1. He already knows.

2. He is the Source of what you need.

I learned the hard way that soaking brings faster healing. Last year, I was sick for an entire week. I could barely lift my head off the pillow, let alone get up to put music on. Holy Spirit kept prompting me to soak and I just didn't want to, so I didn't. He later revealed to me that had I spent that time with Him, I would have been healed much sooner.

Let this encounter be more than just in your mind. You can even do this at work or driving in your car. As peace returns to your mind and heart, turn your attention back to Him, "*Thank You, Father, Your strength is making me strong. Thank You that you are giving me wisdom and understanding.*"

If a scripture comes to mind, look it up and ask Holy Spirit to give you deeper revelation or understanding. Ask Him why He is revealing it to you at this time. Let your heart, mind, will, and emotions be open to His presence.

5. **Expect visual impressions or pictures on the canvas of your brain.**

Holy Spirit will use your mind, the place where you envision things (your imagination station) to give you pictures during this time of soaking. Your imagination is God's gift to you. As children, a lot of us shut our imaginations down because someone told us to stop daydreaming or to pay attention. Well, our imagination is the main way God speaks to some people. Not everybody gets a picture, though. Some people get an impression; others hear music, while still others may hear an audible voice. God communicates with everyone differently, but I firmly believe He enjoys using our imaginations.

- If you see something that you don't understand, just ask Him. Be like a child. Ask tons of questions! Ask about those pictures or impressions. God doesn't get mad because we ask Him a million and one questions. I believe He's quite thrilled when we are interested in what's going on with Him and His plans.

Don't be discouraged if it doesn't seem like it's working the first time, two, or twelve. Make the commitment. Take the first step - a step of faith.

"I WANT to do this. I want to find out how to be intimate with God on a daily basis and let Him live His life through me!"

We begin in faith, with determination to continue trying until we discover and encounter God on every level of our lives. That's not easy, because there are things that fight against it. We have to get our minds renewed to the fact that GOD WANTS TO COMMUNICATE WITH US. GOD WANTS TO BE IN RELATIONSHIP WITH US. God really DOES want to spend time with us! Go back to Psalm 139:13-14, where God talks about how we are "*fearfully and wonderfully made.*" Most of us don't believe that. Because if we did, we would live our lives so very differently.

Remember, there is no set time for soaking. The focus is not on the event, but on the presence of God. Once you are immersed, saturated, and marinated, you take Him with you! When your time of soaking is over, it doesn't mean you leave and the Holy Spirit stays. He goes with you because He is in you (1 John 4:4). The more you soak, the more His presence is on you and the more you have to give. Our experience with soaking, allows others to encounter Him. That's why we need to soak.

Soaking is a dedication: "*God this time is just for you.*"
Soaking is an invitation: "*God do what you want to do in me.*"
Soaking is an expectation: "*Thank you Father for what you are accomplishing in me as I rest in you.*"

Soaking is a Psalm 23 experience. He makes us to lie down in green pastures and He leads us by still waters. He restores our soul. As part of the restoration process, we might laugh, cry, or shake as the Holy Spirit works in us.

Holy Spirit might give us a vision or bring a memory to our minds that He wants to heal. Often we enter into a deep rest. Perhaps we may fall asleep. Even if we don't feel like anything is happening, by faith, we believe that the Lord is working in our spirit. Jesus declared,

> "*If you abide in Me, and My words abide in you, ask whatever you wish, and it will be done for you. My Father is glorified by this, that you bear much fruit, and so prove to be My disciples*" ~ John 15:6-8, NASB

The key to bearing fruit as a Christian is abiding in the Lord. Soaking gives you an opportunity to "abide" in Jesus, allowing His words and His Spirit to abide in you. THIS is how we make a difference in the world. THIS is how we live as ambassadors of the Lord Jesus Christ. THIS is how we lead exceptional lives, different from non-believers! Try it! What can it hurt? Step out in faith and let the God of the universe touch you in places no one has ever touched before. He wants intimacy with you! Do YOU want intimacy with Him?

THE KEY TO BEARING FRUIT AS A CHRISTIAN IS ABIDING IN THE LORD. SOAKING GIVES YOU AN OPPORTUNITY TO "ABIDE" IN JESUS, ALLOWING HIS WORDS AND HIS SPIRIT TO ABIDE IN YOU.

Chapter Twenty-Two

Dad

"Because he loves me," says the Lord, "I will rescue him; I will protect him, for He acknowledges my name."
~ Psalm 91:14

It was two days after Christmas in 2013. I was visiting my parents and we had just returned home from dinner. All of us were in our "jammies" and getting settled in to watch a little TV together. Mom had just asked the question, *"Who's going to fall asleep first?"* We were teasing each other that the first one to fall asleep would be videotaped and placed on YouTube.

Dad got up from his recliner and I noticed an odd exchange between my parents as my mom asked my dad, *what was wrong?* Dad responded with, *"Nothing. I'm just going to get a pop."* I shrugged my shoulders and then got myself comfortable under the quilt and started watching TV.

He came back a minute or two later and sat down in his recliner. This time, I noticed that he sat on the edge and didn't scoot back into a reclining position - not really thinking much about it except that I noticed it. Two minutes later, my dad says, *"I think I need to go to the ER."*

Mom says, *"What?"* and I said, *"Are you serious?"*

Dad replied *"Yes,"* as he grabbed his chest. Our world changed in the blink of an eye as we jumped up to get dressed and head to the local hospital.

You see, this wasn't our first rodeo with this. My dad had his first open heart surgery - triple bypass - when he was only 45 years old. Ten years later, he had his second open-heart surgery, which involved a quadruple bypass and back in 2010, he was diagnosed with lung cancer and had the entire right upper lobe of his lung removed. Not to mention, my youngest brother, David had his first heart attack at the age of 31, has had two more in the next five years with four cardiac stents and a pacemaker. My middle brother, Chris had his first heart attack this past year and received five cardiac stents.

Mom and I are both nurses, we are very knowledgeable and well-versed in caring for cardiac emergencies because we have been through it so many times in the past - on the job and within our family.

This time was different. We ALL knew it.

I asked dad if he wanted to go by ambulance and he ADAMANTLY refused. We didn't argue because we knew we could get him there faster, although, I struggled knowing that if my dad went into cardiac arrest on the way, there was NOTHING we would be able to do about it → in the natural that is.

As soon as we got into the car, I was driving and mom was in the back seat with my dad, I asked my mom to start praying and being the amazing woman that she is, she replied, "*I already have been.*" However, I NEEDED her, to pray out loud. Fear was very real and very present in that car! At this point, I'm pretty sure fear was winning. I needed the atmosphere to change. I needed to feel God's peace. I needed to believe that God was going to take care of my dad, but what I got was silence. I waited another minute or two and then I just started praying out loud. At first, I prayed in English, but after a few minutes, I knew that I didn't really know how or what to pray for, so I switched to my heavenly language.

It kept me calm and helped us to arrive there safely. By the time we arrived at the ER (about 20 minutes after the pain started), the pain was getting worse and he needed to get some relief.

I sent mom in to begin the registration process and commanded dad to wait in the car until I got a wheelchair. He knew better than to cross me! My plan worked though. By the time we got into the ER, the triage nurse was finishing his last patient and took us straight back to room #5. Two male nurses met us there and began the cardiac work-up on my dad. The tension in the room was so tight. The fear was so overwhelming and palpable. I really struggled with standing back and allowing the ER nurses to do their job because I knew that I could do it faster and better, not that they had done anything wrong, of course. They were efficient and kind, but after being an ER nurse for fifteen years and doing this for other families, I wanted the honor and privilege of doing it for MY family.

However, since I knew that I could not, I stepped out of the room and started making some phone calls and texting my prayer warrior friends. Somewhere deep down inside of who I am, I knew this was a bad scenario and I wasn't sure that my dad was going to make it this time, but I didn't want to go there. I am a believer and MY God heals, so I was going to fight tooth and nail to keep my dad from going down like this!

I walked back in the room to find BOTH my dad AND mom crying. Dad was so scared. He knew he was dying and it broke my heart. I had never seen my dad cry before, EVER! It became so real. Fear was in THAT room and he was winning. NOT ON MY WATCH! I got my iPhone out and turned on some healing soaking music by Julie True and just really fought to worship and soak the atmosphere with God's presence.

About an hour or so after we arrived, dad was still in a lot of pain and mom and I were both struggling with the situation. Thankfully, we have an amazing family and incredible prayer warriors in both our churches and within our circle of friends.

They were right there in the trenches interceding on our behalf, loving us from afar and assisting us in bringing Jesus into the situation. We needed every one of those prayers because we knew that this was as much of a spiritual battle as it was a physical one, maybe even more spiritual than we realized.

The ER physician confirmed what we all already knew-- my dad was indeed having another heart attack. Ninety minutes after everything started, my dad was still struggling with intense chest pain and we were doing all we knew to do to help bring him comfort. When all of a sudden, my mother heard an audible voice that she was sure we all heard that said, "***Enough! Get your hands off of my boy!***' The atmosphere changed in that very moment. Peace filled the room and my dad's pain immediately subsided. I saw a large angel standing at the door to his room, holding a sword in battle pose and I could feel the room becoming more and more crowded, even though the same number of people had been in the room the entire time. The angels were filling that room in the spirit realm.

Within minutes, I could see my dad visibly relax and the pain subsided. All I could do was praise Jesus! I knew that He had stepped in to bring comfort to my dad. It was an amazingly calming experience. Fear lost! He was escorted from the room and could not touch us the rest of the weekend.

They finally started him on some IV drips to treat what was going on in the natural - things like Nitroglycerin, Heparin, and Integrilin were all infusing through his IVs. This made the nursing side of me very happy that something was finally being done in the natural. It was like God stepped in and got everyone doing what they should have been doing from the beginning.

Dad was finally transferred up to the Intensive Care unit where he would wait another two long days before he was further evaluated. I remember just feeling the love of God pouring into me like never before, so much so, that this is what I wrote on Facebook:

"Sitting here in the ICU next to my dad and pondering all that 2014 is going to hold - amazed at how grateful I am to be a trained ER nurse and grateful that today is not the day for my dad to leave this earth and neither is tomorrow, next week, next month, or next year! I'm also grateful for the amazing family He put me into and the AMAZING friends He has surrounded me with! But most importantly, I am thankful that MY God holds me in the palm of His hand, will never leave me nor forsake me (Hebrews 13:5; Deuteronomy 31:6), and has a definite plan for my life (Jeremiah 29:11) AND loves me in spite of my weaknesses and failures and is my best friend! Hallelujah!"

Sunday afternoon, the cardiologist stopped in to see my dad, 36 hours post event. He informed us that he would perform another cardiac catheterization on my dad ***sometime*** in the afternoon on Monday. That is, until my mother spoke up and alerted him to the fact that my dad was still having intermittent chest pain that wasn't being controlled by his current plan of care. With this new revelation (for some reason the doctor was not aware of this), the doctor then stated that he would do my dad's catheterization first thing Monday morning.

It has only been until recently that I have been able to even really talk about this, let alone type it out for the world to hear because my heart was so filled with bitterness and anger at the lackadaisical care my father received from this doctor. Holy Spirit has taken me through a repentance and forgiveness process that has finally freed me from the fear and anger I was feeling during that time. He's kind of awesome like that.

Monday morning came and my mother and I arrived early to be there to support my dad. There was no way he was going to have anything done without us knowing and understanding the results as soon as possible. At 0715, the transport team came to take my dad down to the catheterization lab. Mom and I went with him, praying along the way that God was going to handle this and that my dad would be filled with peace.

They took him into the room and began the procedure. A cardiac catheterization is a procedure used to figure out how well the heart is working (My dad has been through a number of them before that day and knew what to expect). A fairly large catheter was inserted through the femoral vein located in my dad's groin. This catheter would then be threaded through the large vessels of the body to just outside of the heart using special x-ray known as angiograms. This allows the doctor to visualize the catheter live as he is threading it up to the heart. Once the catheter is in the appropriate location, the doctor will inject dye that is visible with the angiogram x-rays and can visually determine what is going on in the heart by taking live video pictures of the vessels and the heart muscle. This is called coronary angiography.

Sometimes, they are able to fix occluded vessels by using a balloon to "smash down" the blockages and open the vessel more, or sometimes they even place a medicated stent that will keep that vessel open. This is called angioplasty. Dad has had a number of stents placed on previous occasions, so we weren't too concerned about him needing a few more. However, like I have been saying since the beginning of this chapter, this time around was so very different from previous occasions.

The doctor came out to tell us that my dad was an extremely complex case (duh!) and was going to need to be transferred to the University of Pittsburgh Medical Center, where there were highly skilled providers, who specialized in the challenging cases like my dad.

A few minutes later, the nurses brought dad out into the hallway to wait for transport back to the Intensive Care Unit. He smiled at us, mom gave him a kiss, and then all of a sudden he became very restless. So, I asked him, "*Dad, what's wrong?*" He replied, "*My chest. The pain is coming back.*"

"*Rate it on a scale from one to 10,*" I asked him. He said it was a 4.

"Let me tell the nurse and see if we can get something for that pain," I replied.

In the short time it took to alert the nurse and for them to bring the medicine, dad's pain had jumped to a 7. The nurse became very concerned and alerted the doctor who decided to take my dad back into cath lab to re-evaluate the situation. This meant my dad was going to have his second heart catheterization that day.

The doctor came back to talk with us about an hour later. He told us that he placed my dad on what is known as an aortic balloon pump because dad's heart was not able to effectively push enough oxygenated blood to itself. That's why dad was having so much pain. An Intra-aortic balloon pump is a machine that helps the heart to pump blood to itself and the rest of the body more effectively. It's made up of two parts:

1. A small balloon that sits in the aorta (largest artery in the body that carries blood from the heart to the rest of the body)

2. A large machine that sits outside of the body

The balloon is inserted through the femoral artery and is threaded up to the aorta in the same manner that the cardiac catheter is inserted. Once in place, it is connected to the machine, which causes the balloon to inflate inside the aorta when the heart relaxes, and immediately before the heart pumps, the balloon is deflated, allowing the blood to flow from the heart. This helps get much-needed oxygenated blood to the heart, making the heart very happy because it doesn't have to work as hard. And since the heart didn't have to work so hard, there wasn't ANY pain, which made my dad VERY happy.

Anyway, the doctor then told us that we needed to start preparing ourselves because my dad was going to need a heart transplant. Whoa! Talk about a punch to the gut. I just watched every emotion that I was feeling, cross my mom's face as he said that. But my mom is an amazing woman of faith and as soon as the doctor walked away, she said, "*I don't think so! The only transplant he is going to get is a supernatural one and I break those cursed words off in the name of Jesus!*" Once she said that, I felt enveloped in a peace that I couldn't understand and it actually chased away the anxiety and fear that was starting to creep back in.

Since the helicopter was grounded by the weather, we had to wait for a critical care ground transport team to come from Pittsburgh. In the meantime, Dad stayed back in the procedure room so that he could be monitored until they arrived. Not many emergency medical ambulances are trained to care for a patient with an intra-aortic balloon pump, so we HAD to wait for the team from Pittsburgh, which is about an hour away. Man, it felt like forever!

Since we weren't able to be with dad for the two hours we waited for the critical care team to arrive, Mom and I decided to grab something to eat, make a few phone calls, and update our family and friends, all while encouraging each other. Both of us are critical care nurses and we knew the situation didn't look very good, but God. That is all we could focus on:

- God

- Placing my dad on the altar

- Believing that God was going to step in and do something miraculous.

The critical care team finally arrived and dad and all of his machines were loaded up in the ambulance. Mom and I gave him a kiss and instructed him to behave. He just smiled, which gave me some comfort. We were so glad to finally be moving and that dad wasn't in any pain at the moment.

[187]

Mom and I made the trek to Pittsburgh together. It felt so good to be there to support my mom and dad. I would never want them to go through this alone. While we were in the waiting room waiting to see my dad, my cousin Jake and his girlfriend showed up to give my dad their support. It was so nice to see them and how it touched both my mom and I very deeply that he stopped by to see my dad while they were visiting friends in the area. It just seemed like everyone knew this time was different.

We finally got to see my dad again and I got to investigate this intra-aortic balloon pump. It was very interesting to hear it whirring in the background, knowing it was helping to keep my dad alive and pain free. I studied that thing like I was going to have to take a test on it or something. I'm sure the poor nurse was ready for me to leave after all of the millions of questions I had about the machine. I had seen a few of these machines in my career, but never really understood how they really worked. Now I do! Dad said he couldn't even tell it was there except that he knew it was keeping him pain free. That helped to keep all of our stress levels at a manageable level.

My Aunt Becky (mom's sister) and her husband (my uncle) Dave made the trip from Virginia to Pittsburgh and arrived just before my dad was going to have his third heart catheterization that day. I know that meant a lot to my dad. It certainly meant a lot to my mom and me. They were such a blessing to us. I will never forget the love and support they poured into our family during this really trying time.

It was finally time for him to have his last procedure of the day. They took him to the cath lab and we got everyone caught up on what was going on. We have amazing family and friends who were praying and joining us in our concern for my dad. This last heart cath took over four hours! The doctor finally came out to talk to us around 10 pm that night. He was able to place two stents and do a little angioplasty in another vessel, but there were so many blockages, he couldn't place a stent in the last vessel. His assessment of the situation seemed pretty grim, but he was honest with us and I really appreciated that about him. He told us that they were going to try to manage dad's condition with medications right now and we would re-evaluate in a few months. We all took a big sigh of relief that dad seemed like he was going to make it this time around.

By this time, it was late, so after we had a chance to see dad and let him know we were still there, waiting and praying, we started the trek back home. It was almost midnight before we all were finally able to settle down to try to get some sleep. We were all pretty tired. This is a part of my Facebook entry for that night (I share it with you so you can see how far I have come and Whose strength I was in).

It's almost midnight as I type this entry - it has been one of the longest days of my life! There were a lot of highs and a lot of lows. We cried and we laughed. We prayed and we stood. We loved and we received more love than we could have imagined. God works that way... my dad is resting comfortably as I type and I am so grateful for that. Because even though it was a long day for me and my family, it was an even longer day for him. Not once did I hear him complain or say why me?

"This man, I know as my father, has essentially had THREE heart catheterizations in one day, actually, in a twelve hour period. His first one knocked us to our knees. The second one placed an aortic balloon pump to help his heart to rest and took away all of his pain. The third one took over four hours and partially fixed the problem.

The news we received was not the best, but was far from the worst. And I believe it was because the hand of God was on my dad. There was a peace and serenity that surpasses all understanding that enveloped us. Things that would have really upset me in the past did not bother me today. I knew that I wasn't standing in my own strength, but I was standing in His and as a result, my family was blessed.

[189]

A miracle happened today. And I believe it is just the beginning of the miracles that God is about to pour out on us. Maybe you don't believe in miracles or that there is a God who is behind them... Just watch our family - God is about to do something amazing and I wouldn't want you to miss it!"

Unfortunately, at about 0130 in the morning, my mom's cell phone rang. We all heard it and automatically jumped up and started putting our clothes on because we all figured something had happened to my dad, but it was not about him. My mom's oldest brother, who had been living in a nursing home for the past ten years or so, had passed away unexpectedly. Seriously? Yes, he did. Seems he developed a fever around 10 pm. He was chatting with staff a little after midnight, and when they checked on him at 0120, he had passed away. No one was happy that Robby died that night, but we were relieved it wasn't my dad.

Thankfully, Becky and Dave stepped up to the plate. They took care of everything at the nursing home, finalized all of the funeral arrangements, and notified the rest of the family of the situation. With the help of my youngest brother Dave, they made all the preparations at the house for everyone who would be coming in for the funeral. What a blessing they were! It was a VERY stressful time for us.

The next morning, after we got to the hospital, the doctors decided Dad was stable enough to remove the aortic balloon pump and moved him to a step down unit, outside of the ICU. This was good news! Dad was progressively getting better or so we thought.

When we arrived on the new unit, the nurses were doing their initial assessments and getting dad situated in his new room. It usually takes 30 minutes to an hour for this to take place, so I suggested that we go to the waiting room to give them time and space to complete this process. Unbeknownst to us, dad began having chest pain again. He said that the pain got so bad that all he could think to do was close his eyes and call out, "*Jesus, Jesus,*

Jesus!" When he did, he said he felt like someone's hand was pushing down on his chest. He opened his eyes so he could push the hands away. There was no one even touching his bed, let alone pushing on his chest.

Within ten seconds or so, the pain was gone! He said that he "*knew, that He Knew, that HE KNEW that Jesus had just touched him and took away the pain*" (Psalm 91:14). What a fabulous testimony of the healing hand of Jesus and a reminder to my dad that He had never left him, nor forsaken him (Hebrews 13:5; Deuteronomy 31:6). There is power in the name of Jesus! (Acts 3:1-16)

The name of Jesus is just another awesome gift that has been given to Believers. Hallelujah! In John 16:23-24, it tells us,

> "*And in that day you will ask Me nothing. Most assuredly, I say to you, **whatever you ask the Father in My name He will give you**. Until now you have asked nothing in My name. Ask, and you will receive, that your joy may be full.*" (emphasis added).

His name gives us authority and power over EVERY evil thing. Sickness HAS to go! Diseases have to go! Poverty has to go! Oppression has to go! Even death has to go! ALL of it has to go in the mighty name of Jesus! When a believer speaks that name, SOMETHING has to happen! Jesus wants us to use His name - "*so our joy may be full*"! (John 15:11)

THE NAME OF JESUS IS JUST ANOTHER AWESOME GIFT THAT HAS BEEN GIVEN TO BELIEVERS.

So many Christians claim to believe in Jesus. Unfortunately, they just don't believe in the power of His name. Since they don't believe in the power of His name, they don't cast out demons or heal the sick (See Mark 16:17-18). Thankfully, my dad believes in the power of that name and wasn't afraid or ashamed to use it. Because He used it, all of heaven stood at attention and were ready to move as directed by Jesus and the pain went away.

On the other hand, you must understand that you cannot use that name or the authority that comes with that name without knowing the Person (Jesus) who holds it. In Acts, chapter 19, Paul was seen casting out demons in the name of Jesus. Some Jewish exorcists thought they could do the same - just by using the name of Jesus. They were in for a rude awakening on their first attempt. Let's look at Acts 19:13-17.

> *13 Then some of the itinerant Jewish exorcists took it upon themselves to call the name of the Lord Jesus over those who had evil spirits, saying, "We exorcise you by the Jesus whom Paul preaches." 14 Also there were seven sons of Sceva, a Jewish chief priest, who did so. 15 And the evil spirit answered and said, "Jesus I know, and Paul I know; but who are you?" 16 Then the man in whom the evil spirit was leaped on them, overpowered them, and prevailed against them, so that they fled out of that house naked and wounded. 17 This became known both to all Jews and Greeks dwelling in Ephesus; and fear fell on them all, and the name of the Lord Jesus was magnified.*

Only Believers are given the privilege of using the name of Jesus; those followers who UNDERSTAND what and Who that name represents. It's not something we just add to the end of a prayer ("in the name of Jesus") because that's what everyone else does. It's what makes that prayer come to pass, the ONLY thing that will cause the answer to that prayer to come forth. The name of Jesus is the key to unlocking and releasing your blessing! It has authority in THREE worlds!

1. In heaven over the angels

2. On earth over us

3. In hell over the devil and his minions

It carries ALL power and authority! Just look at Philippians 2:9-11.

> **9** *"Therefore God also has highly exalted Him and given Him the name which is above every name, **10** that at the name of Jesus every knee should bow, of those in heaven, and of those on earth, and of those under the earth, **11** and that every tongue should confess that Jesus Christ is Lord, to the glory of God the Father."*

****

Anyway, Mom and I finally got to see him and he just didn't look very good to me, but I was afraid to discuss it with my mom. It had been such a long few days and I just wanted to celebrate that he was out of the ICU, off the aortic balloon pump, and currently pain-free. We all needed something positive to focus on.

A few hours later, my dad STILL didn't really seem to be doing much better in the natural. The nurse came in to take his vitals and the pulse oximeter (which measures oxygen concentration of the blood and the pulse) couldn't pick up my dad's pulse or oxygen concentration. We are taught in nursing school that if you are unable to get a reading on the machine, there is more than likely something wrong with the machine. So, the nurse went to get another machine. That one wouldn't pick it up either and a touch of anxiety hit my heart as she left to find yet another machine. It's NEVER two machines that don't work! One of them might not work, but usually not two and definitely NOT three!

I reached out and grabbed my dad's wrist to discover that I couldn't find a radial pulse by palpation. I tried for like five minutes. Then I grabbed his other arm and couldn't find one there, either. To make matters worse, my dad's hands were ice cold. Definitely NOT a good sign! When the body begins to shut down, it pulls all of its excess blood and heat, etc., from the extremities to the core of the body. I think you can see where my mind was taking me.

His nurse finally returned and was able to successfully get some numbers to come up on the machine, but I didn't believe them. I knew what was presenting itself, but I couldn't bring my heart or mind to acknowledge it. There was NO WAY that my dad was going to go out like this! I wanted to pray into the situation, but I just couldn't - I felt empty, alone, and afraid that I was going to lose my dad that night.

Mom and I were really tired and dad slept most of the day. Since we had a house full of people, we decided to head home a little earlier than usual. It was difficult for me to leave - I was struggling to believe that my dad would make it through the night, but I refused to say that out loud! However, that didn't stop the emotional torment that I was struggling with on the inside as exhibited in my next Facebook post:

"Tonight I feel the need to update my friends and family on Facebook about what has been happening with my dad over the past few days. I think very carefully before each and every post as I consider why I am posting this time.

My first thought was that there are a LOT of people on here who care about me and my family and just might be a little bit interested in the information, but if I want to be honest with myself, it's really because I feel the weakest that I have ever felt in my life and quite frankly, I need you. I need your faith.

My dad is only 62 years old and is fighting for his life. There's no easy way to put it. We are tired and weary and we are struggling... I am being very honest here - very vulnerable here.

We believe that God wants to perform a supernatural miracle - We really do, but we need His strength and power to endure, and constant encouragement and reminding that HE (Jesus Christ) still sits on the throne - until the manifestation is complete. We need you faith-filled believers to stand in the gap for us - it's a very humbling and challenging place to be...

God is in control! We know this! We also know that God did not bring this on my dad, but He can and He will turn this around for my dad's good (Romans 8:28).

Am I afraid of my dad dying? No. I know where he's going (1 Thessalonians 4:13-14; 1 John 5:13) and to Whom He belongs (John 10:27-30; Romans 8:16). I am a tad uncertain of what my world would be like, though, without him in it - and more importantly, I believe God would be more glorified by his living than by his death (in my humble opinion!)

With that said, I do not know what God is doing behind the scene. What I DO know is that He IS moving behind the scenes!! He IS strengthening us all the time, especially when we have a moment of lapse and hear that voice trying to convince us that God isn't there or that He won't move on our behalf.

NEWS FLASH: God is moving even when we can't see or feel Him! He IS moving! He's not surprised by this and has a perfect plan for my dad's life. AND most importantly, He loves us right where we are and He WILL be glorified! Why? Because He deserves ALL the glory and honor and so much more!

In the morning, my dad is headed back to the cath lab - we are praying for wisdom, knowledge, and compassion for the medical team, but more importantly, we are praying for God's miraculous power to show up because that is what HE has promised - all of his promises are Yes and Amen and also for God to be glorified!!"

My mind was struggling against everything my heart was telling me. In the natural, my mind knew that there was no way my dad was coming back from this. But my heart kept hearing Jesus tell me,

"Rachel, I got this! I REALLY do! Your dad's story doesn't end here. Trust me! Lean on me! I got this!"

Those words had been enough for me over the past few days, but on this day, I was struggling with doubt AND unbelief.

So, I cried out to Him and said,

"I want to believe You, Jesus, more than my words can say, but I'm struggling here. I'm really struggling. Can you give me something,... just a little something to show me that you are there, something I can hang my faith on, please?"

He first surrounded me with some amazing friends, intercessors, and encouragers, not to mention my amazing family. We had people all over the world praying for us and with us. It was an amazing place to be! They filled us with so much love, support, and encouraging words.

In fact, one example I want to share involved our dear friends from Deep Water Ministries International and their church, The River Valley Life Center (www.rivervalleylifecenter.com) in Lancaster, Ohio. They were in the middle of their New Year's Day service when I texted Cindy Teagarden to update her on the current status of my dad.

Cindy showed my text to Pastor Paula who alerted Pastor Paul immediately. They stopped the service and Pastor Paul had Mike Teagarden come to the front and stand in for my dad, as he and the rest of the congregation prayed for and lifted my dad up to the throne of God. They all texted me later telling me that they could FEEL the response of the Holy Spirit - the atmosphere changed, and they all knew that my dad was going to be all right.

My eyes are filling up with tears, EVEN now, as I remember how much love and support we received from so many around the world. Holy Spirit used EVERY one of them to bring the peace, comfort, and strength we needed to get through such a challenging event in our family.

That night, as I was laying down to sleep, I could feel His wonderful arms wrapped around me. He was encouraging and reminding me of His promises and that He was still working behind the scenes and the final product was going to be something beautiful.

You see, I have a REAL relationship with Jesus! We talk, laugh, and cry... sometimes I yell, even though He never does. That night I told Him that I was struggling with my faith, with my hope, with my understanding of Who He is and that I have never felt so weak in all my life. He told me that it was ok. He told me that He had me and would never leave me. He reminded me of how much He LOVES to make weak things strong (Isaiah 40:31; 1 Corinthians 2:2-5; 2 Corinthians 12:10). I reminded Him that I really wanted to believe Him and I was struggling with that; and I asked Him to give me something, anything, to hold onto, to remind me that His promises are yes and amen! (1 Corinthians 1:20)

He just smiled and said, "*I AM here and I got this! Just trust in me!*"

I said, "*Ok, I will trust You,*" and went to sleep AND slept like a baby for the first time since all of this started.

Dad was scheduled for another heart catheterization in the morning. Mom and I got there very early to support him again and we found something amazing! Dad was sitting on his bed, talking, smiling, with good color, and WARM hands! I never thought something could feel as wonderful as those warm hands and bounding radial pulse!

> "*The effective, fervent prayer of a righteous man avails much.*" ~ James 5:16

I could NOT stop smiling! Jesus didn't just give me something little, He gave me something BIG! He ALWAYS gives us way beyond what we ever ask for! (Ephesians 3:20) Thank You, Jesus!

The heart catheterization was canceled because they had discovered the night before that my dad had received too much fluid the previous day and his weakened heart was unable to handle it. However, they were able to get things under control with medications through the night. Praise the Lord!

My dad was a new man, and because he was, the next day, mom and I were able to attend the funeral of her brother who had passed away a few days earlier. Family and friends joined mom and me the following day after the funeral and were amazed at how well dad was doing. He was able to talk sports with my cousin Sam, visit with his sister, mom's friend Sally, and my Uncle Dave.

My dad was discharged from the hospital the very next day, eight days after this nightmare started. So many miracles happened during this time and although, at times, it "felt" like God wasn't there, He TOTALLY WAS!

Holy Spirit started the transformation in us (Dad, Mom, and me) a long time ago. I like to say it all began when the three of us started learning what the Bible has to say about healing, but the truth of the matter is the Holy Spirit had been preparing us for this time even before we were created in our mothers' wombs. Holy Spirit was not the least bit surprised that my dad suffered a heart attack that was aimed at claiming his life on that December day in 2013. He knew I would be visiting my parents that week and that there would be some serious spiritual warfare needed to win this battle on my dad's behalf.

He knew we were going to need spiritual warriors to get in the trenches with us and He brought them into our lives, one at a time over the years (You know who you are). He knew that each one of us and each one of those who dug in with us would be in the right place in their walk with Him to provide the support that we needed. Holy Spirit knew as He continued to pursue MY heart, what steps I needed to take to be where I was able to battle for my dad's life.

That's what this book is all about. It's about how Holy Spirit took my hand and led me into this amazing relationship with Him. This particular event was happening to my dad and in a way, it was happening to me. Holy Spirit used it to show me, how far He had already taken me. He showed me my new foundation for the next part of my journey with Him. He lovingly took away the doubt and strengthened my faith.

It hasn't been easy and I struggled a lot. Holy Spirit is so patient, gentle, loving, and kind. He knows when to push, when to convict, when to teach, and when to comfort and love. When I started this journey with Holy Spirit, I was filled with doubts and questions. "*How could all of this be real?*" I often asked myself, "*How can it be truth?*" I couldn't get my mind out of the way, but I decided to keep trusting, to keep believing, to keep making room for Holy Spirit to effectively change me to be more and more like Him. What an awesome privilege to be changed precept by precept (Isaiah 28:9-10).

As Joyce Meyer is known to often say, "*I've got a long way to go. But at least I'm not where I used to be!*" It's really not about the destination, but the journey and how we handle each step. So, let me ask you:

- Are you willing to get to know the Holy Spirit for Who He is?

- Are you willing to spend time in His presence and allow Him to guide you?

- Are you willing to get out of your head and learn to live from your heart - that place where the Holy Spirit resides on the inside of you?

I pray that you answer all of those questions with an astounding, "*YES!*" I know MY life has never been the same since the day that I invited Him to enter my heart to change me. I would love for you to experience the same thing.

Chapter Twenty-Three

Wrapping it ALL Up!

"Truly, truly I say to you, he who believes in me will also do the works that I do; and greater works than these will he do because I go to the Father." ~ John 14:12

Before I actually write the concluding paragraphs of this book, I wanted to give you an update on my dad. Nine months after the life-altering event that nearly took his life, he had another heart attack. Thankfully, he did well and it was much smoother than the previous event. THEN, exactly one year and one day later, my dad developed chest pain and shortness of breath while he and I were watching the Pittsburgh Steelers play football against the Cincinnati Bengals. Mom had told him before she went to bed that there were to be no more repeats of last year and that he was to behave and be calm while watching the game. We all had a good laugh and dad told us he had no desire to repeat last year.

Unfortunately, 90 minutes later, after two episodes of diarrhea, dad developed chest pain and shortness of breath. Once again, I had to wake my mom from a deep sleep to tell her that dad was requesting to go to the ER. This was becoming too much of a habit and we were definitely NOT amused! We got dad to the hospital and of course, he was admitted again. He needed another heart catheterization and we decided to skip doing that at the local hospital and requested to be transported to Pittsburgh, where the doctors knew my dad and how complicated his case was.

To make a long story short, dad got to Pittsburgh, had his catheterization, got another stent placed in an artery in his heart, and was discharged home the next day. However, this heart catheterization was performed by a partner of my dad's primary doctor, who was on vacation. Turns out Dr. Toma had been performing a new procedure using the heart catheterization that was able to clear an already 100% blocked artery! Mom and I couldn't believe it! We were so excited because we realized that this was a divine appointment, an answer to many, many prayers!

The doctor spoke to my dad about it, but dad wasn't as nearly as excited as mom and I were. He didn't really understand what would happen during this new procedure and he didn't want to be a guinea pig (not that I could blame him). So, he was discharged home to think and pray about things. Dr. Toma called mom at home, explained everything to her, and then made an appointment to discuss it again in the office with both of my parents. I explained to my dad that he was the perfect candidate because:

1. He already knew what God had to say about healing,

2. He had a gazillion people praying for him,

3. AND we already knew that God was going to use this procedure to perform another miracle.

Who better to choose than my dad?

Dad finally agreed to the procedure and had his Right Coronary Artery (RCA) completely cleared and held open with five stents AFTER it had been completely blocked for 18 years. He recovered very well and was discharged the next day. He said it's the first time in a long time that the heaviness in his chest wasn't there. Praise the Lord!

You see, I believe that God is healing my dad just like he said he would. He's giving him a new heart and a new lease on life. Some of you might be thinking or saying, "*but the doctor did it!*" And, you would be right, sort of. I believe that God can heal in any manner He chooses. If He wants to heal my dad through the doctor's hands (who He gave the knowledge and training to), then so be it. This procedure has **only** been utilized on patients in the past year. The doctor who performed it is labeled as one of the leading practitioners using this new technique. He has an 85% success rate, and just happens to be the partner of my dad's doctor who practices in a small city in Southwestern Pennsylvania of all places. Coincidence? I don't think so. God-ordained is what I choose to believe. My God is a healer and He is so faithful to do what He promises.

He is faithful. He is ALWAYS faithful and His promises are Yes and Amen (2 Corinthians 1:20). I am so grateful to have had the grace to handle and understand the situation, and the ability to stand and fight for my dad's life.

Anyway...

I've spent a lot of time thinking and praying about how to finish this book. The Holy Spirit has become such an important part of my life and I wanted to find just the right words to tie everything together. You see, churches of today spend a lot of time talking about God, the Father, and God, the Son (Jesus). They raise and lift them up, as they should, but they speak casually about the Holy Spirit. Many Christians don't know what it really means to have the Holy Spirit. There just isn't a whole lot of preaching or teaching about Him.

Therefore, most believers do not understand or realize that He (the Holy Spirit) is VITAL to our Christian walk.

The Holy Spirit is Who helped Jesus while He was on the earth. I know what some of you are thinking, "*Whoa, wait a minute. Jesus is God's Son. He was perfectly capable of doing all of the wonderful things He did."* Yes, He was, but think about this for just a minute. Jesus came to earth, not only to make a way for us to return to the Father, but He did it in such a way that we could see how WE are expected to live. He set His divinity aside (Philippians 2:6-8) and lived life on earth as a mere mortal and human. He was still 100% God while He was 100% human. Jesus went from being the Glory of Glories in Heaven to being a human being who was put to death on the cross.

> **6** *"Who, being in the form of God, did not consider it robbery to be equal with God,* **7** *but* **made Himself of no reputation, taking the form of a bondservant, and coming in the likeness of men.** **8** *And being found in appearance as a man, He humbled Himself and became obedient to the point of death, even the death of the cross"* ~ Philippians 2:6-8 (emphasis added)

In the ultimate act of humility, the God of the universe became a human being and died for His creation. He chose to live out of His humanity, powered by the Holy Spirit, so He could show us how to do the same. How else could we follow His direction given to us in John 14:12?

> *"Truly, truly I say to you, he who believes in me will also do the works that I do; and greater works than these will he do because I go to the Father."*

Don't you think it would be incredibly unfair of Jesus to expect us to do the same works He did without us being God? That is why God sent His Son - not only to save us from the pit of hell, but also to show us what living life in His Kingdom is supposed to be like. He did it **By the power of the Holy Spirit!** In Romans 8:11, Paul tells us,

> *"The same Spirit that raised Jesus from the dead dwells in us."*

Think about it. If the Holy Spirit empowered Jesus' ministry and this same Holy Spirit lives inside of us, then why are we not living the same life as Jesus did? Why are we not seeing the same miracles, signs, and wonders that happened whenever Jesus was present?

THE CHURCHES OF TODAY ARE SO AFRAID OF BEING WRONG, THEY WILL KEEP ANYONE FROM FINDING OUT WHAT'S RIGHT. THEY WOULD RATHER KEEP WITH THEIR CHERISHED TRADITIONS (LIKE THE PHARISEES) THAN TO SUBMIT TO THE HOLY SPIRIT.

I believe there is a very simple answer to this question, an answer that has been sitting right in front of our faces all along. We do not know nor do we understand Who the Holy Spirit is and how He works in and through us for His glory. We now have the privilege to cast out demons, heal the sick, and raise the dead, just like Jesus did! The churches of today are so afraid of being wrong, they will keep anyone from finding out what's right. They would rather keep with their cherished traditions (like the Pharisees) than to submit to the Holy Spirit.

Jesus lived differently than the rest of the world (John 18:36), just like we are supposed to do (John 17:14). He was not accepted in this world and came in total opposition to the religious systems that were present in that day. Just as I believe He would be in total opposition to most churches today. The Pharisees and the Sadducees are the ones who put Jesus on the cross because He had a power (the Holy Spirit) that they did not understand. They didn't like the fact that Jesus walked around casting out demons, healing the sick, and raising the dead. The religious people of today are crying about the same thing!

Jesus proclaimed in Luke 4:18-19,

> **18** *"The Spirit of the LORD is upon Me, Because He has anointed Me To preach the gospel to the poor; He has sent Me to heal the brokenhearted, to proclaim liberty to*

*the captives and recovery of sight to the blind, to set at liberty those who are oppressed; **19** To proclaim the acceptable year of the LORD."*

THAT, my friends, is good news! That is the type of news that gets people excited to know Jesus! Listen, the world today is tired of just hearing about Jesus. They want to SEE Him in action. How can they see Him in action? Through God's children who are empowered by the Holy Spirit to do the same things that Jesus did and to live the kind of life Jesus lived!

LISTEN, THE WORLD TODAY IS TIRED OF JUST HEARING ABOUT JESUS. THEY WANT TO SEE HIM IN ACTION.

Jesus still lives!
Jesus still saves!
Jesus still provides!
Jesus still protects!
Jesus still heals!

Jesus still sets people free through us, empowered by the amazing Holy Spirit! Jesus never changes (Hebrews 13:8).

Do you know what happens when the Holy Spirit walks into a room? The very atmosphere changes! Sickness and disease can no longer stay, poverty must go, depression and anxiety must vacate the place, and oppression bolts for the door (Acts 10:38).

When the Holy Spirit walks into the room, you KNOW He is there. There is peace. There is joy. There is love. There is patience. There is kindness. There is goodness. There is faithfulness. There is gentleness and there is self-control (Galatians 5:22-23). When you tell me that you had an encounter with God (Father, Son, OR Holy Spirit), but you are not stirred up on the inside and showing it on the outside, then I will question the validity of your statement.

[206]

You see, when the Holy Spirit walks into the room, everything changes. He comes to meet every single need you have. That is His heart. He wants to provide for your EVERY need! When He walks into the room, He wants to heal you from that terminal disease just like the woman with the issue of blood (Matthew 9:18-26). When He walks into the room, He wants to provide for you, just like He fed the 4000 (Matthew 15:29-39; Mark 8:1-13) and the 5000 (Matthew 14:13-21; Mark 6:30-44; Luke 9:10-17; John 6:1-15). When the Holy Spirit walks into the room, He shows mercy to the sinner (Luke 19:2-9) and so much more. Whatever your situation is, the Holy Spirit can handle it.

Impossibilities become possibilities (Jeremiah 32:27; Matthew 19:26; Mark 10:27; Luke 1:27) whenever He gets involved because the devils words are powerless. What other people have to say falls by the wayside because when the Holy Spirit walks into the room, into the situation, EVERYTHING changes! What we need in our churches today is to allow and welcome the Holy Spirit when He walks into the room.

How many of you are just waiting for Him to show up?

Well, guess what? If you are born again and Spirit-filled, when YOU walk into the room, Holy Spirit walks into the room, too! I know some of you are saying, "*Rachel, that's blasphemous! YOU are not the Holy Spirit!*" You're right. I'm not. However, 1 John 4:4 says,

> "*You are of God, little children, and have overcome them, because* **He who is in you is greater than he who is in the world.**" *(emphasis is mine)*

When you walk into the room, He gives YOU power and authority. WHAT? Oh Yes, He does! Look at what Luke 10:19 has to say about that.

"Behold, I (Jesus) give you (the believer) the authority to trample on serpents and scorpions, and over all the power of the enemy, and nothing shall by any means hurt you."

All this time you have been wanting and waiting for the Holy Spirit to show up, and all along, He has been waiting for you! You just need to believe it and then receive it before He will bring the manifestation into your life! You are the only one stopping Him from manifesting in your life. When you come to the realization that you CAN and WILL do all of the things that Jesus did because of the amazing gift of the Holy Spirit

ALL THIS TIME YOU HAVE BEEN WANTING AND WAITING FOR THE HOLY SPIRIT TO SHOW UP, AND ALL ALONG, HE HAS BEEN WAITING FOR YOU!

that Jesus left behind when He ascended to be with the Father, then and only then will you experience heaven on earth. Then and only then, will you allow all of heaven's power to arrive on the scene with the power to save, to heal, to deliver, and to set the captives free.

THIS is what this book was about for me. I was pursued by the God of the Universe. I accepted Jesus as my Lord and Savior. He, in return, gave me the gift of salvation. He gave me the gift of grace. He came to live on the inside of me and gave me the gift of the baptism of the Holy Spirit. He has been teaching me, loving me, and showing me what His kingdom is supposed to look like on the earth. He has gifted me with the ability to write, to share, and to teach.

Learning about the Holy Spirit has been a struggle for me. However, it didn't need to be. That is what I want to share with you, so that maybe, you won't have to struggle as much as I did. I want this book to provoke you to search for the Holy Spirit, to learn about Him, to learn from Him, and to be in relationship with Him. I'm not foolish enough to believe that you would accept what I have learned in this book as the truth and quite frankly, I don't want you to. Search the Word of God. I have included a

LOT of scriptures for you to look up, study, and meditate on. Become like the Bereans. Prove or disprove what I have written. Either way, I know that it will bring you into an encounter with the God of the Universe and He will make all things plain to you.

He didn't make encountering the Holy Spirit complicated at all. WE have made it complicated. It's so easy, even small children can encounter Him. In fact, many of them encounter Him easier and more often than adults because they understand the basics. They understand simple. They understand truth. The Holy Spirit is NOT hiding from us , nor is He far away, wondering if we will EVER figure it out! He is constantly drawing us into a deeper relationship with Him.

Are you willing to let go of your preconceived notions about Who He is and allow Him to change your world? What are you waiting for? Step out in faith and take the ride of your life with the One Who knows you and loves you! Trust Him. He is faithful.

If you have found this book helpful:

- Please head on over to amazon.com and leave a supportive review, letting future readers know how this book could bless them, too!
- Share it with your friends!
- Visit me at www.fromaheartofstone.com and sign up to receive emails about my upcoming projects

I truly appreciate the time you took to read my first book, "*From a Heart of Stone*". It is my sincere desire that my personal journey will leave you with an insatiable hunger for ALL things pertaining to the Holy Spirit and that you, too, will develop a life-changing relationship with Him.

For information on how to:

- invite Rachel to speak at your next conference, Bible Study, seminar, church, etc.
- to schedule a healing school, miracle service, or retreat
- share what Holy Spirit is doing in your life

Please contact Rachel at info@rachelgodfrey.org

To leave a review on Amazon.com

1. Go to www.amazon.com
2. Search for "*From a Heart of Stone*" by Rachel Godfrey
3. Scroll to the bottom and click on "**Write a Customer Review**"
4. Rate the book (out of 5 stars) and write your review

To be noted: *You do not have to purchase the book at Amazon to write a review. However, you must have an amazon account. Thank you, in advance, for your positive review!*

APPENDIX A

Asking Jesus into Your Heart

Don't freak out when you read this, but all of us members of "Club Christian" (aka Christians)... we're all messed up!

Yes, Christians make bad decisions too - And, like everyone else, our poor decisions make God sad.

Are you running for the hills yet? I hope not!

Here's the cool thing: God's dialed into all the junk we fall into - whether you're in Club Christian or not. He sees beyond our facade, right into our heart and wants to offload all the nasty goop each of us carry around. From guilt and shame, to hurt and hatred, He stands ready, holding an empty trash can for you to dump your junk and goop into. THEN He replaces it with peace and forgiveness. He wants a deeper, closer relationship with each of us.

Why? Because He loves us. He loves YOU!

We all have goop. And, we all have junk - it's that stuff we call sin. God says, "***All have sinned and fall short of the glory of God.***" ***(Romans 3:23)*** (BTW, that goes for both Club members and non-Club members)

OK, so rewind the clock to some 2000 years ago. God sends His only son, Jesus. Jesus cruised around doing all kinds of wildly awesome miracles while on Earth. But His #1 accomplishment came when He died for all our junk - our sin. The Bible says "But God demonstrates his own love for us in this: "***While we were still sinners, Christ died for us.***" *(Romans 5:8)*

Here's the best part. (Drum roll, please...)

In true, totally AWESOME fashion, Jesus rose from the dead and now He lives in heaven at the right hand of the Father. He offers us the gift of eternal life - of living forever with Him, in heaven, if we accept Him as our Lord and Savior.

> Jesus said, "***I am the way, the truth, and the life. No one comes to the Father except by Me***." **(John 14:6)**

Now, if you're reading this and thinking you might want some too, it's easy to start your journey and accept Him as your Lord and Savior. Are you ready?

This is going to be cool! OK, just relax your heart and mind for a second, close your eyes and say this quick prayer:

"Lord Jesus, I believe you are the Son of God. Thank you for dying on the cross for my sins. Please forgive my sins and give me the gift of eternal life. I ask you into my life and heart, to be my Lord and Savior. I want to serve you always. Thank You, Jesus! Amen!"

Did you pray that? If so, I would **LOVE** *to hear about it... I won't do anything weird like show up at your house. But I would like to pray for you and answer any "what now?" questions you might have.*

Be blessed and welcome to the family!!

~ Rachel
info@rachelgodfrey.org

APPENDIX B

50 Things The Holy Spirit Does

1. He convicts the world of sin, righteousness, and judgment (John 16:8).

2. He guides us into all truth (John 16:13).

3. He regenerates us (John 3:5-8; Titus 3:5).

4. He glorifies and testifies of Christ (John 15:26; 16:14).

5. He reveals Christ to us and in us (John 16:14-15).

6. He leads us (Rom. 8:14; Gal. 5:18; Matt. 4:1; Luke 4:1).

7. He sanctifies us (2 Thess. 2:13; 1 Pet. 1:2; Rom. 5:16).

8. He empowers us (Luke 4:14; 24:49; Rom. 15:19; Acts 1:8).

9. He fills us (Eph. 5:18; Acts 2:4; 4:8, 31; 9:17).

10. He teaches us to pray (Rom. 8:26-27; Jude 1:20).

11. He bears witness in us that we are children of God (Rom. 8:16).

12. He produces in us the fruit or evidence of His work and presence (Gal. 5:22-23).

13. He distributes spiritual gifts and manifestations (the outshining) of His presence to and through the body (1 Cor. 12:4, 8-10; Heb. 2:4).

14. He anoints us for ministry (Luke 4:18; Acts 10:38).

15. He washes and renews us (Titus 3:5).

16. He brings unity and oneness to the body (Eph. 4:3; 2:14-18).

17. He is our guarantee and deposit of the future resurrection (2 Cor. 1:22; 2 Cor. 5:5).

18. He seals us unto the day of redemption (Eph. 1:13; 4:30).

19. He sets us free from the law of sin and death (Rom. 8:2).

20. He quickens our mortal bodies (Rom. 8:11).

21. He reveals the deep things of God to us (1 Cor. 2:10).

22. He reveals what has been given to us from God (1 Cor. 2:12).

23. He dwells in us (Rom. 8:9; 1 Cor. 3:16; 2 Tim. 1:14; John 14:17).

24. He speaks to, in, and through us (1 Cor. 12:3; 1 Tim. 4:1; Rev. 2:11; Heb 3:7; Matt. 10:20; Acts 2:4; 8:29; 10:19; 11:12, 28; 13:2; 16:6,7; 21:4,11).

25. He is the agent by which we are baptized into the body of Christ (1 Cor. 12:13).

26. He brings liberty (2 Cor. 3:17).

27. He transforms us into the image of Christ (2 Cor. 3:18).

28. He cries in our hearts, "Abba, Father" (Gal. 4:6).

29. He enables us to wait (Gal. 5:5).

30. He supplies us with Christ (Phil. 1:19, KJV).

31. He grants everlasting life (Gal. 6:8).

32. He gives us access to God the Father (Eph. 2:18).

33. He makes us (corporately) God's habitation (Eph. 2:22).

34. He reveals the mystery of God to us (Eph. 3:5).

35. He strengthens our spirits (Eph. 3:16).

36. He enables us to obey the truth (1 Pet. 1:22).

37. He enables us to know that Jesus abides in us (1 John 3:24; 4:13).

38. He confesses that Jesus came in the flesh (1 John 4:2).

39. He says, "Come, Lord Jesus" along with the bride (Rev. 22:17).

40. He dispenses God's love into our hearts (Rom. 5:5).

41. He bears witness to the truth in our conscience (Rom. 9:1).

42. He teaches us (1 Cor. 2:13; John 14:26).

43. He gives us joy (1 Thess. 1:6).

44. He enables some to preach the gospel (1 Pet. 1:12).

45. He moves us (2 Pet. 1:21).

46. He knows the things of God (1 Cor. 2:11).

47. He casts out demons (Matt. 12:28).

48. He brings things to our remembrance (John 14:26).

49. He comforts us (Acts 9:31).

50. He makes some overseers in the church and sends some out to the work of church planting [through the body] (Acts 20:28; 13:2).

APPENDIX C

Healing Scriptures for Meditation

How do we know whether it's God's will to heal us or not? What others say about it makes little difference. What did He say about it?

If God never intended healing for us, He spoke many words which He did not mean. Below are many promises of the Father – direct and indirect – regarding Healing.

Old Testament

God said...

1) *I am the Lord that heals thee (Exodus 15:26).*

2) *Your days shall be one hundred and twenty years (Genesis 6:3).*

3) *You shall be buried in a good old age (Genesis 15:15).*

4) *You shall come to your grave in a full age like as a shock of corn comes in his season (Job 5:26).*

5) *When I see the blood, I will pass over you and the plague shall not be upon you to destroy you (Exodus 12:13).*

6) *I will take sickness away from the midst of you and the number of your days I will fulfill (Exodus 23: 25, 26).*

7) *I will not put any of the diseases you are afraid of on you, but I will take all sickness away from you (Deuteronomy 7:15).*

8) *It will be well with you and your days shall be multiplied and prolonged as the days of heaven upon the earth (Deuteronomy 11:9, 21).*

9) *I turned the curse into a blessing unto you, because I loved you (Deuteronomy 23:5 and Nehemiah 13:2).*

10) *I have redeemed you from every sickness and every plague (Deuteronomy 28:61 and Galatians 3:13).*

11) *As your days, so shall your strength be (Deuteronomy 33:25).*

12) *I have found a ransom for you, your flesh shall be fresher than a child's and you shall return to the days of your youth (Job 33:24, 25).*

13) *I have healed you and brought up your soul from the grave; I have kept you alive from going down into the pit (Psalm 30:1, 2).*

14) *I will give you strength and bless you with peace (Psalm 29:11).*

15) *I will preserve you and keep you alive (Psalm 41:2).*

16) *I will strengthen you upon the bed of languishing; I will turn all your bed in your sickness (Psalm 41:3).*

17) *I am the health of your countenance and your God (Psalm 43: 5).*

18) *No plague shall come near your dwelling (Psalm 91:10).*

19) *I will satisfy you with long life (Psalm 91:16).*

20) *I heal all your diseases (Psalm 103:3).*

21) *I sent My word and healed you and delivered you from your destructions (Psalm 107:20).*

22) *You shall not die, but live, and declare My works (Psalm 118:17).*

23) *I heal your broken heart and bind up your wounds (Psalm 147:3).*

24) *The years of your life shall be many (Proverbs 4:10).*

25) *Trusting Me brings health to your navel and marrow to your bones (Proverbs 3:8).*

26) *My words are life to you, and health/medicine to all your flesh (Proverbs 4:22)*

27) *My good report makes your bones fat (Proverbs 15:30).*

28) *My pleasant words are sweet to your soul and health to your bones (Proverbs 16:24).*

29) *My joy is your strength. A merry heart does good like a medicine (Nehemiah. 8:10; Proverbs 17:22).*

30) *The eyes of the blind shall be opened. The eyes of them that see shall not be dim (Isaiah 32:3; 35:5).*

31) *The ears of the deaf shall be unstopped. The ears of them that hear shall hearken (Isaiah 32:3; 35:5).*

32) *The tongue of the dumb shall sing. The tongue of the stammerers shall be ready to speak plainly (Isaiah 35:6; 32:4).*

33) *The lame man shall leap as a hart (Isaiah 35:6).*

34) *I will recover you and make you to live. I am ready to save you (Isaiah 38:16, 20).*

35) *I give power to the faint. I increase strength to them that have no might (Isaiah 40:29).*

36) *I will renew your strength. I will strengthen and help you (Isaiah 40:31; 41:10).*

37) *To your old age and gray hairs I will carry you and I will deliver you (Isaiah 46:4).*

38) *I bore your sickness (Isaiah 53:4).*

39) *I carried your pains (Isaiah 53:4).*

40) *I was put to sickness for you (Isaiah 53:10).*

41) *With My stripes you are healed (Isaiah 53:5).*

42) *I will heal you (Isaiah 57:19).*

43) *Your light shall break forth as the morning and your health shall spring forth speedily (Isaiah 58:8).*

44) *I will restore health unto you, and I will heal you of your wounds saith the Lord (Jeremiah 30:17).*

45) *Behold I will bring it health and cure, and I will cure you, and will reveal unto you the abundance of peace and truth (Jeremiah 33:6).*

46) *I will bind up that which was broken and will strengthen that which was sick (Ezekiel 34:16).*

47) *Behold, I will cause breath to enter into you and you shall live. And I shall put My Spirit in you and you shall live (Ezekiel 37:5, 14).*

48) *Whithersoever the rivers shall come shall live. They shall be healed and everything shall live where the river comes (Ezekiel 47:9).*

49) *Seek Me and you shall live (Amos 5:4, 6).*

50) *I have arisen with healing in My wings (Malachi 4:2).*

New Testament

God said...

51) *I will, be thou clean (Matthew 8:3).*

52) *I took your infirmities (Matthew 8:17).*

53) *I bore your sicknesses (Matthew 8:17).*

54) *If you're sick you need a physician. (I am the Lord your physician) (Matthew 9:12 & Exodus 15:26).*

55) *I am moved with compassion toward the sick and I heal them (Matthew 14:14).*

56) *I heal all manner of sickness and all manner of disease (Matthew 4:23).*

57) *According to your faith, be it unto you (Matthew 9:29).*

58) *I give you power and authority over all unclean spirits to cast them out, and to heal all manner of sickness and all manner of disease (Matthew 10:1 & Luke 9:1).*

59) *I heal them all (Matthew 12:15 & Hebrews 13:8).*

60) *As many as touch Me are made perfectly whole (Matthew 14:36).*

61) *Healing is the children's bread (Matthew 15:26).*

62) *I do all things well. I make the deaf to hear and the dumb to speak (Mark 7:37).*

63) *If you can believe, all things are possible to him that believes (Mark 9:23; 11:23, 24).*

64) *When hands are laid on you, you shall recover (Mark 16:18).*

65) *My anointing heals the brokenhearted, and delivers the captives, recovers sight to the blind, and sets at liberty those that are bruised (Luke 4:18; Isaiah 10:27; 61:1).*

66) *I heal all those who have need of healing (Luke 9:11).*

67) *I am not come to destroy men's lives but to save them (Luke 9:56).*

68) *Behold, I give you authority over all the enemy's power and nothing shall by any means hurt you (Luke 10:19).*

69) *Sickness is satanic bondage and you ought to be loosed today (Luke 13:16 & II Corinthians 6:2).*

70) *In Me is life (John 1:4).*

71) *I am the bread of life. I give you life (John 6:33, 35).*

72) *The words I speak unto you are spirit and life (John 6:63).*

73) *I am come that you might have life, and that you might have it more abundantly (John 10:10).*

74) *I am the resurrection and the life (John 11:25).*

75) *If you ask anything in My name, I will do it (John 14:14).*

76) *Faith in My name makes you strong and gives you perfect soundness (Acts 3:16).*

77) *I stretch forth My hand to heal (Acts 4:30).*

78) *I, Jesus Christ, make you whole (Acts 9:34).*

79) *I do good and heal all that are oppressed of the devil (Acts 10:38).*

80) *My power causes diseases to depart from you (Acts 19:12).*

81) *The law of the Spirit of life in Me has made you free from the law of sin and death (Romans 8:2).*

82) *The same Spirit that raised Me from the dead now lives in you and that Spirit will quicken your mortal body (Romans 8:11).*

83) *Your body is a member of Me (I Corinthians 6:15).*

84) *Your body is the temple of My Spirit and you're to glorify Me in your body (I Corinthians 6:19, 20).*

85) *If you'll rightly discern My body which was broken for you, and judge yourself, you'll not be judged and you'll not be weak, sickly or die prematurely (I Corinthians 11:29-31).*

86) *I have set gifts of healing in My body (I Corinthians 12:9).*

87) *My life may be made manifest in your mortal flesh (2 Corinthians 4:10, 11).*

88) *I have delivered you from death, I do deliver you, and if you trust Me I will yet deliver you (2 Corinthians 1:10).*

89) *I have given you My name and have put all things under your feet (Ephesians 1:21, 22).*

[223]

90) *I want it to be well with you and I want you to live long on the earth. (Ephesians 6:3).*

91) *I have delivered you from the authority of darkness (Colossians 1:13).*

92) *I will deliver you from every evil work (2 Timothy 4:18).*

93) *I tasted death for you. I destroyed the devil who had the power of death. I've delivered you from the fear of death and bondage (Hebrews 2:9, 14, 15).*

94) *I wash your body with pure water (Hebrews 10:22; Ephesians. 5:26).*

95) *Lift up the weak hands and the feeble knees. Don't let that which is lame be turned aside but rather let Me heal it (Hebrews 12:12, 13).*

96) *Let the elders anoint you and pray for you in My name and I will raise you up (James 5:14, 15).*

97) *Pray for one another and I will heal you (James 5:16).*

98) *By My stripes you were healed (I Peter 2:24).*

99) *My Divine power has given unto you all things that pertain unto life and godliness through the knowledge of Me (2 Peter 1:3).*

100) *Whosoever will let him come and take of the water of life freely (Revelation 22:17).*

101) *Beloved, I wish above all things that you may prosper and be in health (3 John 2).*